A PHILOSOPHER LOC
RELIGIOUS LIFE

What is happiness? Does life have a meaning? If so, is that meaning available in an ordinary life? The philosopher Zena Hitz confronted these questions head-on when she spent several years living in a Christian religious community. Religious life – the communal life chosen by monks, nuns, friars, and hermits – has been a part of global Christianity since earliest times, but many of us struggle to understand what could drive a person to renounce wealth, sex, children, and ambition to live a life of prayer and sacrifice. Hitz's lively and accessible book explores questions about faith, sacrifice, asceticism, and happiness through philosophy, stories, and examples from religious life. Drawing on personal experience as well as film, literature, history, biography, and theology, it demystifies an important element of contemporary culture and provides a picture of human flourishing and happiness that challenges and enriches modern-day life.

ZENA HITZ is a tutor at St. John's College, Annapolis, Maryland, where she teaches across the liberal arts. Her acclaimed book *Lost in Thought: The Hidden Pleasures of an Intellectual Life* (2020) was widely discussed and reviewed in a number of prominent periodicals, including the *Wall Street Journal*, the *Chicago Tribune*, and the *Irish Times*.

A Philosopher Looks at

In this series, philosophers offer a personal and philosophical exploration of a topic of general interest.

Books in the series

A PHILOSOPHER LOOKS AT

THE RELIGIOUS LIFE

ZENA HITZ

CAMBRIDGE
UNIVERSITY PRESS

CAMBRIDGE
UNIVERSITY PRESS

Shaftesbury Road, Cambridge CB2 8EA, United Kingdom

One Liberty Plaza, 20th Floor, New York, NY 10006, USA

477 Williamstown Road, Port Melbourne, VIC 3207, Australia

314–321, 3rd Floor, Plot 3, Splendor Forum, Jasola District Centre,
New Delhi – 110025, India

103 Penang Road, #05–06/07, Visioncrest Commercial, Singapore 238467

Cambridge University Press is part of Cambridge University Press & Assessment,
a department of the University of Cambridge.

We share the University's mission to contribute to society through the pursuit of education,
learning and research at the highest international levels of excellence.

www.cambridge.org
Information on this title: www.cambridge.org/9781108995016

DOI: 10.1017/9781108993159

First published 2023

Printed in the United Kingdom by TJ Books Limited, Padstow Cornwall

A catalogue record for this publication is available from the British Library.

Library of Congress Cataloging-in-Publication Data
NAMES: Hitz, Zena, 1973- author.
TITLE: A philosopher looks at the religious life / Zena Hitz.
DESCRIPTION: New York, NY, USA : Cambridge University Press, 2022. |
    Series: A philosopher looks at | Includes bibliographical references and index.
IDENTIFIERS: LCCN 2022030675 (print) | LCCN 2022030676 (ebook) | ISBN 9781108995016
    (paperback) | ISBN 9781108993159 (epub)
SUBJECTS: LCSH: Religion–Philosophy. | Religious life.
CLASSIFICATION: LCC BL51 .H58 2022 (print) | LCC BL51 (ebook) | DDC 204–dc23/eng/
    20220815
LC record available at https://lccn.loc.gov/2022030675
LC ebook record available at https://lccn.loc.gov/2022030676

ISBN 978-1-108-99501-6 Paperback

For the staff workers of Madonna House, past, present, and future

and

in memory of Raymond Richard Ames, 1964–2022

E che brindis replicati
Far vogliamo al Dio d'amor.

CONTENTS

ACKNOWLEDGMENTS

This book was written at the invitation of my editor, Hilary Gaskin. I am grateful for her imaginative insight in suggesting the topic. Even more, I am grateful for the encouragement and support that she has freely offered since olden times, when I was a young scholar in classical philosophy, before I went off on desert adventures and before I dreamt of writing for a general audience.

My three years in Madonna House dramatically shaped my life as a teacher as well as my work as a writer. The loving friendship of their staff began several years before my long-term arrival in 2011, and has continued without interruption since I left the community and was released from my promises in 2015. The manuscript was drafted during a long stay as a guest at the new branch of Madonna House in Salem, Missouri, Marian Acres, and I am grateful beyond words for the support and hospitality of the staff there: Patrick Stewart, Carol-Ann Gieske, Fr. Zachary Romanowsky, Fr. Denis Lemieux, and Trina Stitak.

My friends in the religious life have also helped me by their example and through their friendship: Fr. John Corbett, O.P.; Sr. Anna Maria Robertson, O.P.; Fr. Michael Sherwin, O.P.; Fr. Thomas Joseph White, O.P.; and in early days, the Sisters of St. Joseph at the Baltimore parish of St. Mary, Star of the Sea, especially Connie, Julie, and Pat.

Fr. Denis Lemieux read the first draft of the manuscript and gave very helpful encouragement and suggestions. Kieran Setiya shared his own forthcoming manuscript with me and read the first parts of mine. Both his conversation and his writing have helped me a great deal in thinking about happiness, activity, and the meaning of life. I have also been lucky to have his advice and support in our common endeavors in public writing. I have been talking to Janice Thompson about the book of Job, God, and suffering since college days. She kindly read and commented on this stage of our conversation, and I owe her for all time for bringing to my attention the wonderful example of St. Catherine of Siena's service to the sick. Pater Edmund Waldstein, O.Cist, generously read the first draft and made the essential suggestion to expand the section on prayer. It is a much better book thanks to his help. Lastly, the anonymous reviewer put me under pressure to clarify my argument and to soften its more counter-intuitive aspects and helped me to correct numerous errors.

I did the reading and research for the book when libraries were strictly quarantined and frequently closed, and it was very difficult to obtain materials. A book grant from the Institute for Humane Studies was essential, as was the kind help in securing library access from Margaret Cabaniss and Carter Snead at the de Nicola Center for Ethics and Culture at the University of Notre Dame.

As the manuscript was in final preparation, my dear friend Rick Ames died after a short and intense battle with gastric cancer. Rick was the first ascetic and desert brother that I knew. Our friendship shaped the way I lived and saw the world, from the time I was an impressionable college freshman and through the decades following. Rick lived chiefly in solitude, with simplicity and with principle. After college he enlisted in the US Army and served in civil affairs units in Bosnia, Afghanistan, and Iraq. He then took up his vocation as a math teacher, taking a long hiatus to nurse his mother through her dementia. He taught math until his death. He loved music, art, and poetry; he shunned notice and notoriety. He might have hated this book, but his stamp lies on it all the same. *Et lux perpetua luceat eam.*

WHAT IS THIS BOOK ABOUT?

In the third century CE, in the village of Coma in Lower Egypt, near to the modern-day city of Beni Suef, Antony grew up in a prosperous Christian family. His parents died when he was a young man, leaving him three hundred fruitful acres. Not long after their death, he walked to church, thinking of how in the book of Acts the disciples sold all they had to live in common, giving to each according to his need. In church, he heard read the gospel of the rich young man. A young man asks what he must do to inherit eternal life, beyond the following of the commandments. Jesus tells him to sell all he has and give it to the poor "so that he will have treasure in heaven," and to follow him. The young man "went away sad, for he had many possessions."[1]

Antony took the gospel as a direct, personal instruction. He sold his family lands, gave away his possessions, and went to live in solitude in the desert. Flocks of disciples chased him into ever more desolate places.[2] His life, written by Athanasius, caused a sensation in late antiquity that lasted at least until the time of Augustine, inspiring religious foundations in the East and the West.

Around the time of Antony's death in the fourth century, a Roman conscript in Gaul named Martin met a beggar on a cold winter's evening. Moved with pity, he cut his own cloak in half with a sword and shared it with him. That night he dreamt he saw Jesus Christ wearing the half of the cloak, and speaking from Matthew 25: "I was naked, and you clothed me." Martin resolved to retire from military life. He renounced his arms and devoted himself to poverty, prayer, and service.[3]

In twelfth-century Italy, Francis, the happy-go-lucky son of a wealthy fabric trader, encountered a beggar and refused him alms. Haunted by his refusal, Francis chased the beggar down, gave to him generously, and vowed never to refuse a beggar again. His vow was tested shortly afterward when he met a leper who begged him for alms. He gave him money according to his vow, and overcoming his natural repulsion, kissed his hand. Francis then heard the voice of Christ speaking from a crucifix to "rebuild his church." Francis sold some of his father's fabric and began to rebuild, stone by stone, a local ruin. His angry father seized him, locked him away for a time, and eventually brought him before the bishop to disinherit him. Francis paid the money he owed and stripped naked down to his hairshirt before all present:

> Until now I called you my father, but from now on I can say without reserve "Our Father, Who art in heaven." He is all my wealth and I place all my confidence in him.

He set out into a life of poverty, naked and penniless, begging for alms, and gathered many followers.[4]

These three men are very famous, but not as neurological zoo animals that might display interesting forms of mental dysfunction. They are famous as Christian holy men, who loved God and sacrificed everything to serve him. What sense can be made of their lives? What good or goods do they pursue? How could that good require such dramatic forms of renunciation?

What does Antony seek in the desert that he could not find on his fruitful acres? What kind of "wealth" does Francis receive from his heavenly father that outweighs the goods and privileges given by his human father? Both Francis and Martin are struck first, not by God directly, but by other human beings. They are overcome by a desire to serve the poor and to share their sufferings. Yet they do not become social workers but dedicate their lives to God. What could dedication mean – and who or what is the God who receives it?

Since the time of Antony, Christian men and women have renounced wealth, ambition, marriage, and childbearing to take up lives of solitude, silence, enclosure, poverty, celibacy, and obedience. They formed like-minded communities and in the wisdom of experience, wrote rules of consecrated life, of which the Rule of St. Benedict is the most famous. Insofar as my book is about the religious life, it is about these institutes – the communities of monks, nuns, friars, sisters, and brothers, as well as hermits and anchorites – that have marked rural and urban landscapes across the world since the early centuries of Christianity.

Religious life is not exclusively Christian. Ascetic lives especially dedicated to the divine are found in Buddhism and Hinduism. Further, something like religious life is suggested in both Jewish and Islamic traditions, by Nazarites such Samson, the Hebrew prophets, and the Muslim anchorites of Ibn Tufayl's *Hayy ibn Yaqzan*. I will acknowledge the broad appeal of religious life – it is, after all, a testament to its broad humanity – but my focus will be on the Christian traditions, as these are the traditions where my ignorance is smallest and with which I have personal experience.

The forms of Christian renunciation vary wildly across both place and time. Europeans think of vast stone cloisters, once seats of great wealth, rich enough to be robbed by Robin Hood. Americans think of the pioneering active orders, the nuns who built schools and hospitals across the wild country; or the Jesuit missionaries, who traveled by foot and canoe into parts of Canada no European had set foot in before, to be tortured and killed by the Iroquois. But Christianity, as we so often forget, is both an ancient and a global religion. It originated in Palestine and thrived in India, Egypt, and Ethiopia before England or Germany ever heard a word of it. Its most ancient churches flourished until recently in Iraq and Syria. Today, as the churches empty in Europe and North America, they grow and flourish in sub-Saharan Africa and Latin America, sending priests into the religious deserts whence their former evangelists came.

The differences in devotion and practice in most of the churches east of Italy hardened in the Great Schism of 1054. As a result, a great family of religious institutes and other forms of religious life lies separate from and often invisible to most Christians of North America and western Europe. North Americans are more likely to be acquainted with the handful of Protestant versions of religious life – the Amish, Mennonites, Quakers, Hutterites, or Bruderhof – than the ancient structures of Orthodoxy or the eastern Catholic rites.

In the Roman Catholic tradition, the religious life developed under more central governance and with a greater devotion to written rules than one might find elsewhere. Even so, it shows enormous variation among active orders (focused on service) and contemplative orders (focused on prayer), mendicants (who beg), clerics (who preach), monastics (who are stable), lay movements (who keep a foot in the world), and private consecrations (virgins, widows, or hermits). Yet the roots of the Roman communities also lie in the deserts of Egypt and Syria, in the desires of those strange pioneers who felt called to leave everything and to follow Christ alone.

The Carmelite tradition, school for the great saints of prayer and sacrifice, Teresa of Avila, John of the Cross, and Thérèse of Lisieux, takes as its founder the prophet Elijah. Elijah, whose life and works are described in the book of Kings, challenged the violently corrupt kings of Israel and slaughtered the prophets of Baal. For fear of his life, he lived in the wilderness, in caves and in the homes of the humble folk who would receive him. He once heard God speak, not in a storm or a wind, but in a "thin sound of silence."[5] He could be recognized by his hairy cloak and leather belt.[6] The leather belt remains perhaps one of the few common markers of a Christian religious.[7]

If I were to write as a historian or sociologist, it would take many thousands of pages to do justice to the enormous variety of religious communities and their influence on Christian life more generally. Fortunately, I am a philosopher, and my gross ignorance, like the ignorance of Socrates, provides opportunities in its defects.

For all of the variety and difference across cultures and time periods, I am persuaded that Christian religious life is one thing. Christian religious, be they hermits, anchorites, monks, nuns, friars, clerics, or consecrated laypeople, be they Catholic, Orthodox, Coptic, Chaldean, Melkite, Maronite, Ruthenian, or Syro-Malabar, all have one thing in common. They renounce the trappings of ordinary human life – like-minded friends, family, freedom of movement, living by one's own judgment, wealth, status, sex, marriage, children – to live for God alone.

As is common in both religious and secular realms, words that might bear the whole meaning of human life can decay into slogans, brittle and meaningless. What does it mean to renounce everything to follow Christ, or to live for God alone? And what could attract someone to such a life? These two questions shape the central inquiry of this book.

Religious life might seem to be a very special way of practicing Christianity. Yet the call of the rich young man that Antony heard is a call to all believers. When the young man "goes away sad," Jesus tells his disciples how difficult it is "to enter the kingdom of heaven" with one's wealth. By choosing not to follow Jesus, the young man loses the distinctive promise to Christians. The core commitments of religious institutes are not different in substance from the Christian life that all Christians are called to lead, no matter their walk of life.

Are all called to live in solitude in the desert? I doubt it. A tension lies between two visions of Christianity, both ancient. In the vision of the Acts of the Apostles (4:32–35) that inspired Antony – where the Christian disciples hold all in common, selling their property to be distributed to the poor – Christians are necessarily distinctive, if not quite as wild as the desert monastics. By contrast, we have the vision of the third-century Letter to Diognetus, where Christians are famously described as "in, but not of the world."[8] Christians have no special language or dress nor any outlandish way of life. Rather, they live as others do – except that they love all human beings, including their persecutors. This tension seems to lie in the Gospels themselves. Christians are encouraged to be both shining lamps on a lampstand and invisible leaven in the dough.

Related to the tension about Christian distinctiveness is a tension in the meaning of renunciation. To "face death each day," as Paul chose, is not to linger on precipices or busy highways but to love without counting the cost, even if the cost is fatal.[9] Giving up everything has not been usually interpreted as giving up clothing. (Francis of Assisi's nudity was only temporary, unlike the holy nakedness of his ancient predecessor, Mary of Egypt.[10]) The desert monastics survived on what plants and insects they could find. Modern monastics, by contrast, may live off their own land and so have nourishment significantly superior in taste and nutrition to any diet known to the world's poor. The concrete meaning of total renunciation varies widely across centuries, times, places, and particular individuals. What, then, is "total" about it?

The challenge to a philosopher of Christianity is to find an account of total renunciation that fits the varieties of Christian holiness, without watering down the radicalism of Christian life. I suggest that the goal is to practice renunciation to the point where it is possible for a given individual to receive as good whatever circumstances offer in a given moment, as chosen or permitted by the divine will. In other words, renunciation counts as total whenever it induces a state of *abandonment*.[11] Abandonment is the central form of Christian freedom. It encompasses the great paradox of Christian flourishing, the happiness in crucifixion, and the exaltation of martyrdom. It is the practical resolution of the "problem of evil," the apparent inconsistency between a loving, all-powerful God and the scope and manner of human suffering.

Because abandonment involves receiving the people and circumstances of daily life as presented by divine providence, it unites one's own will with the will of God. Abandonment is then a way to be joined with God, and is the form of divine union available to human beings on this side of death. It is the ultimate expression of the love for God and prepares the way for the knowledge of God promised to us after death, as in the words of Paul: "At present we see indistinctly, as in a mirror; but then we shall see face to face."[12]

If these thoughts are on the right track, the difference between religious life and the life of an ordinary Christian lies not in any core principle but in its social role. Religious life sets out to communicate the central teaching of Christianity. The traditional personal mode of Christian communication works via the flesh and blood, bodies and souls, of living human beings who have undertaken a way of life.

Those ways of life can and should display variety, in the spirit of Paul's attempt to become "all things to all people."[13] The creative devotion of religious develops a vast landscape of different approaches to prayer and service as well as ways of re-imagining, in light of Christianity, the conditions of our carnal humanity – eating, drinking, forms of shelter, and modes of dress. In turn, the variety of inessentials attracts in its humble way the variety of human hearts to the teaching of the Gospels and the call to charity as the end of mortal life.

Compare the role of the prophet in the communities described in the Hebrew Bible. The prophet lives apart and brings the words and the distinctive power of God to his or her community. The living apart is not a living for oneself but in order to define and preserve an iconic role within the community of believers. The prophet is not meant to be the only true believer or the only true follower of the laws of God. But whatever the failures of the individual prophet, his or her life is an icon, a signpost when the path is lost, a light in darkness, a point of orientation; or, as in the Hebrew Bible, a standard against which failure is measured.

Often enough, religious life fails by its own standards. Its failures can be minor imperfections or can bear catastrophe to individuals or communities. In their power to build, to nurture, to maim, or to destroy, religious communities resemble our families and communities of origin. I keep the focus of this book on the best cases, not out of blindness or ignorance – or worse, to manage the reactions of my readers – but because we know what things are by their best instances. What practical means can be taken to ensure the best cases and to avoid catastrophes is a very interesting question, but not one I am qualified to tackle.[14]

Indeed, there are many ways in which I am not qualified to write the book that follows. I rely in part on my own experiences joining a religious community. Yet I left the community only six months after making my first promises of poverty, chastity, and obedience. What I know of religious life has necessary limitations: There are levels of growth and understanding which I never reached. Fortunately, my central interest is the practice of total renunciation, which belongs in a special way to the entry-point of a religious community. In the Roman church, entry and its defining sacrifice are associated most closely with the novitiate, the period of training after a trial period but before the making of vows or promises. The novitiate takes one to two years; mine lasted eighteen months. In my attempts to explain total renunciation, I am describing something which I practiced only for a time, and so which I may well fail fully to understand.

The community I lived with and joined for a short time was not a community of nuns and monks, strictly speaking. The Madonna House community, based in eastern Ontario, is among what are called in the Roman Catholic Church, "new communities" or "lay movements." These groups arose in the twentieth century to bridge the divide between the formal cloistered orders on the one hand and the Christians of the world on the other: those who marry, bear children, and work in the world. No habits are worn at Madonna House, and they pray only a few of the traditional offices. They do not go by "sister" or "brother," nor do they take special names. More strikingly perhaps, men, women, and priests, all vowed to celibacy, live in community with one another, sharing meals, liturgies, and occasional work projects. Madonna House resembles a monastic community in that its members do not pursue conventional careers, but unlike a monastery, no enclosure is observed. The door is open to guests who share in community life.

I use as many examples from as many contexts as I can in this book. I am promiscuous with my sources, drawing on novels, films, and stories as well as on formal histories or theological treatises. I do so to illustrate the universal appeal of religious life, its humanity, as well as its flexibility for different circumstances and cultures. In doing so, of course, I reach well beyond any pretense I might have to an expert understanding of these sources, their home communities, or their historical or cultural richness. My hope is that this will make it easier to be philosophical, as the title suggests: to find what is universal, true, relevant, and human in the practices of Christian religious life.

Religion is not primarily a matter of the intellect, but a matter of the heart: of what and who and how one loves. Like most loves, the love for God is sparked by a personal encounter, perhaps with God directly, but more often, with some other human being who loves God. It travels from heart to heart. Nonetheless, it is hardly irrational. What we love follows from what we see and what we understand. Just as in other loves, we can long for something after glimpsing only a shadow of its garment; and just as in other loves, the more we know of our beloved, the greater our love becomes. We love our infant children in ignorance; as their lives unfold, so does the scope and shape of our devotion.

Religious life is unusual in Europe and North America these days, but it is not niche. It is the central icon of Christian spirituality, the life and death of Christ, cast in living flesh and blood. This spirituality offers the heights of human excellence, and thereby, human happiness – and demands at the same time total renunciation. Central to this spirituality is Christian freedom, liberty from the bonds of selfishness, abandonment to the divine will, not for its own sake, but for union with God and communion with one's neighbor.

I hope that the book will have speculative interest to philosophers, especially those studying virtue, happiness, the meaning of life, transformative experience, and aspiration. But I also hope that it will hold the attention of anyone seeking insight into his or her own life and the choices that structure it.

Introduction
Renunciation and Happiness

In my first year of academic teaching, I decided to enter the Roman Catholic Church. It was a simple decision: I wanted a religion, and I had already tried the respectable academic religions, Judaism and Anglicanism. I began the six-month class at the local parish to prepare me for baptism, confirmation, and Communion, to take place at the long liturgy the night before Easter.

I didn't mind receiving simple teaching along with ordinary parishioners. It was refreshing to be exposed to wisdom that anyone with some life experience could understand. To me it was like stripping off the inessentials to live for a time in my human skin. Nor did the dogmatic requirements present any difficulty to me; I'd been in academic philosophy for years. My graduate program had been free-wheeling and ambitious: Theories built in minutes, or years, crumbled in an instant on a counter-example. One could never predict the conclusion that might issue from the baroque machinery of argument.

It was evident to me that the exercises of analytic philosophy were a wonderful training in clear thinking but faced serious shortcomings as a means of discovering the truth. I knew people far more intelligent than I was who denied the existence of everything except indivisible corpuscles, or who thought that if I could have had pork chops

1

for breakfast, there was a real place where I did have pork chops for breakfast. Why shouldn't I believe in a three-personed God, born as a man to a virgin, who died, was resurrected, and returned to us under the forms of bread and wine?

Two weeks before Easter, I heard Genesis 22, Abraham's sacrifice of Isaac, read at Sunday Mass. The voice comes from nowhere. The voice which called Abraham to travel to the land of Canaan, which has promised him a son for decades, which grants his desire only after his wife is past menopause, now makes a different kind of request. The voice asks Abraham to take "your son, your only son, whom you love" and sacrifice him on a mountaintop.

The ancient author takes us step by step. Abraham arises early and packs his donkey – with the wood for the burnt offering and the knife. As he travels with his son up the mountain, the boy notices that they carry every supply for a sacrifice – "but father, where is the animal?" The narrator only reports Abraham's evasive reply: "God will provide the sacrifice, my son." We are left to imagine how Isaac's words cut his father to pieces, just as we the listeners are cut to pieces.

Like the intervening angel who saves Isaac's neck in the end, the narrator sympathizes with our horror. But it is easy to feel the horror without feeling the sympathy. So it was. When I heard the story read at Sunday Mass, my peace was destroyed. I went into a panic.

The seed of my distress was the following thought: God had absolute power over me without the least concern for my happiness. And happiness – the happiness of learning and friendship, the hoped-for happiness of marriage and children, was everything to me. How could it be otherwise? Consequently, how could I worship such a God? What sacrifice would God ask of me? I related my panic to my pastor, and he recommended to me the life of Thérèse of Lisieux, a French Carmelite nun of the late nineteenth century, dubbed the "Little Flower" for her childlike joy.

Thérèse's mother died when she was a child, and her father suffered from serious mental illness. The young girl insisted on entering Carmel as soon as possible, begging for permission to enter before she met the minimum age of sixteen. Carmel is among the most severe of the religious orders, requiring real poverty, silence, and sacrifice. For Thérèse, it also meant enduring the scorn of the other nuns, colored by ignorance, for her preternatural intelligence and determination. Thérèse died of tuberculosis at the age of twenty-four, after suffering two years of complete emptiness in which it seemed there was no God at all.

The story did not console me. Yet somehow I traveled through the last days before my baptism, one step at a time, respecting the difficulty but unwilling to let it determine my decision. In the end, the crisis was not resolved so much as it was moved out of focus. I had a nice job, after all, along with opportunities to travel, volunteer work, hobbies, and friends. It was easy to think that no voice had yet come out of nowhere instructing me to sacrifice what I loved most. Easy, but false, as my initial reaction to Abraham suggested that I had, in fact, heard just such a voice.

When a few years later I felt drawn to enter religious life myself, the specter of Abraham and Thérèse sacrificing everything human for an invisible God returned to haunt me afresh. As I gave away most of my possessions and said goodbye to my friends and family, it felt like dying. It seemed I was a ghost haunting the empty vestiges of my previously vivid life. Worse: it was supposed to feel that way.

Azer Youssef Atta, who became Pope Kyrillos VI of the Coptic Church, entered a monastery in 1928 as a handsome, successful young man of twenty-five. As his biographer tells it, after a night of vigils and prayers,

> Azer lay on his back on the ground before the relics of the saints, crossing his hands on his chest, as though he were dead in a coffin. It was his funeral. According to the rite, the Scripture readings and hymns were chanted in the "mournful" tone, and over the body of the reposed young novice, the Litany of the Departed was prayed. Having died to his old self, the novice now arose as a monk of Christ. After cutting his hair five times in a cruciform pattern, the abbot clothed Azer in his monastic cassock, head covering, and leather girdle. Azer was no more. Henceforth he was Fr Mina el-Baramousy.[1]

My spiritual director at Madonna House, a former dentist, was less ceremonious. "If you didn't come here to die," he said, "you came for the wrong reason."

Baptism is death, as Paul writes in the letter to the Romans: the death of Christ that is the condition for his resurrection.[2] Likewise, religious profession is death. Paul describes his own life as a disciple as a daily embrace of

4

death.[3] Death in Christianity is ambiguous: There is the good death, the death to self, the death to "the world" – that is the locus of ambition, competition, and the pursuit of wealth and power – which leads to life. There is also the bad death, the death that for Paul is the fruit of sin and rebellion. Baptism, like religious profession, is a good sort of death. We might be inclined to sugarcoat and look to the promised goodness. Alas: at least on the surface, Christianity reverses conventional terms of "good" and "bad."

Consider the true story told in the 2010 film *Des Hommes et des Dieux* (*Of Gods and Men*). A community of Trappist monks in Algeria in the 1990s lies under threat from Islamist rebels who have been murdering Europeans. The monks must discern whether to go back to France or to stay with the local Muslim villagers, with whom they have lived for decades. Over the course of a few weeks, one by one, each of the monks determines to stay, refusing to return to the life they left behind in France. In a dramatic confrontation, the abbot tells one of the more frightened and reluctant men, "You have already given up your life!" The abbot means that when the man made his initial commitment to the monastery, he offered his life as a sacrifice to God. In other words, he compares joining a monastery to accepting one's imminent murder by hostile strangers.

When I was discerning religious life, both from the outside and within the Madonna House community, I could not swallow the prospect of total renunciation, even unto a violent death. I could not even bear to give up my large collection of books. What was drawing me on if it was not death or violent death?

My attraction to religious life grew in intensity corresponding to my discontent with the life I was leading. I was restless, bored, and frustrated with the tedium of a moderately successful academic career. I had had enough of teaching for money, studying for status, loving in order to advance myself. I was tired of using myself and being used; I wanted to live a life that could not be bought or sold. I had studied the philosopher Aristotle for years, without living out his central ethical insight: that happiness consists in human activities pursued for their own sake. I still wanted to think and learn and teach, but I wanted to do so out of love for human beings, not to score points in an invisible game where victory always slipped just out of reach.

For me, then, the draw to religious life was partly alienation from my own work. I experienced that alienation as a kind of superficial selfishness, as though my academic life mattered only for its most immediate and thrilling forms of sweetness: publications, citations, promotion, and praise. These goals – which governed my life unconsciously, not explicitly – provided temporary satisfaction but long-term nausea, like eating too much candy.

I sought to remedy my selfishness by adding on new activities, various forms of volunteer service in the community: hospice work, literacy tutoring, and finally jail ministry. That broke my life into fragments: loving my neighbor here, earning money there, scrabbling for status here, simple acts of service there. I kept putting on and off my human skin, as if I couldn't make up my mind about it. I wanted a life that was dedicated, wholehearted, and governed by what I aspired to hold as my deepest values, love of God and love of neighbor.

We say that someone has dedicated their life to mathematics, or to music, or to ending the achievement gap, or to teaching sewing or gardening, or to the good of the town of Peoria, Illinois. We mean that they gave everything they had to it. We do not seem to mean that literally everything they did was mathematical or musical. But we might mean that everything that doesn't contribute to that end is discarded – say, if my basket-weaving hobby is useless to the cause, no more basket-weaving. Or we might mean something less stringent: I discard everything incompatible with that end. I can keep on basket-weaving, but if I want to dedicate my life to Peoria, I cannot move away – unless, of course, my presence is Peoria's biggest problem.

God is not the only person who demands wholehearted commitment without compromise. So does anyone we seek to love unconditionally. If I claim true devotion to my romantic partner but hedge my bets by keeping channels open with my previous lovers, or if I keep investigating real estate in lands where I know he will not live, I am lying, either to myself or him or both. My love is conditional until I throw away the exit routes. I am meant to love my child without condition; if my other activities compete with my child's needs, or worse, threaten their safety, I have failed to love them as I should.

The clearest violation of wholeheartedness is corruption. A police officer wears the uniform of law, order, and the protection of the innocent but takes bribes from criminal rackets on the side. A teacher or priest, dedicated to the care of the young, secretly preys on them. Both Plato and Aristotle claimed that the ban on private property that made the ancient Spartans so austere and admirable was too harsh to be borne: Their citizen-soldiers kept secret treasuries and hoarded gold in private.[4] We call corruption "hypocrisy" after the Greek word for acting, putting on a mask. The corrupt lead a double life behind a false front, not only for public consumption but as part of the corrupt person's own self-deception. The real danger of living a lie is not so much getting caught in it as beginning to believe the lie oneself.

Total dedication and wholeheartedness are among the strongest themes of the New Testament. The voice of God, spoken through John in the book of Revelation, tells the church of Laodicea:

> I know your works, I know that you are neither cold nor hot. I wish you were either cold or hot. So, because you are lukewarm, neither hot nor cold, I will spit you out of my mouth. For you say, "I am rich and have no need of anything," and yet do not realize that you are wretched, pitiable, poor, blind, and naked.[5]

Lukewarmness is grounds for rejection by God. The kingdom of heaven is like a pearl of great price for which one sells everything. The sons of Zebedee are fishing on the Sea of Galilee when they meet Jesus; they leave their boats and nets to follow him. The good in question, however we understand it, is worth all of our other goods – or rather, it is incomparably more valuable than anything and everything else.

Lukewarmness seems different from corruption: It is more lack of commitment, half-heartedness, than hypocrisy. Why is it condemned so harshly? The Revelation passage does not only condemn lukewarmness; it diagnoses it. We say, "I am rich and have no need of anything," not realizing that we are in fact wretched and vulnerable. Lukewarmness and compromise suggest a double life, built around a central fantasy of self-sufficiency, where one's vulnerability and weakness are kept private.

Consider Oedipus, the central character of Sophocles' tragedy *Oedipus Tyrannus*. His fame is for his unusually sordid crime, which can obscure his function as an illuminating human type, an "everyman." He begins the play self-assured, accomplished, in control; he has won the crown by his ingenuity in solving the Sphinx's riddle; he rules from his own resources. At the end of the play, which takes place over a single day, he is blind and wretched, an exile, the object of fear and revulsion. The difference is the discovery of the truth of who he is: a person who was born, like all of us, in ignorance of his parentage, who makes only choices that make sense at the time and ends up doing the very things he has dedicated his life to avoiding. What seemed to be in his power, avoiding this fate, was in no way in his power. That his fate is to murder his father and marry his mother is only a detail. His fundamental helplessness, the blindness he is subject to in virtue of being a human being, is just like ours.

It was that fundamental helplessness that I caught a glimpse of when hearing the story of Abraham and Isaac. I feared that if I were not in charge of my happiness, I would not attain it. Such fears were fed by my relative wealth and success. Wealth is dangerous: it provides the illusion of dominance over my surroundings. If I can replace something in my household if I simply don't like its looks; if I can order a car and driver whenever my feet are tired, or fly to Rome whenever I crave pasta carbonara, or order a warm blanket at the first chill of winter, I develop illusions about myself. Even worse, if I can transform a landscape with my enterprise, whether by building or by destruction, if I have the power of life or death over others, I begin to imagine that I am a different sort of being than I really am, a godlike one that makes reality when I open my mouth or raise a single finger. Yet ultimately my control is extremely limited, as Oedipus learned, by the luck of circumstances and by inescapable forms of human ignorance. Wealth can seem to make these contingencies shrink, but they cannot be eliminated. Dependence and blindness are core realities for every human being.

The illusion of dominance and control that wealth and comfort bring can be subtle – I was, after all, very grateful for the comfort and luxury I lived in, and the gratitude softened my sense of entitlement. Yet once I had the luxury of high status, it was central to the way I thought of myself. It was deeply painful even to leave the academic Olympus of Princeton University, where I had finished my degree, to move on to a merely excellent job. Even my initial interest in religion showed signs of the illusion of self-sufficiency. It is the epitome of lukewarmness to treat God as one choice among others, as an added benefit to one's already wonderful, flourishing life. No wonder the story of Abraham unsettled me so.

———

How did Oedipus, or any of us, come to be so tragically divided between strength and vulnerability, as the Revelation passage suggests, to believe oneself to be powerful when one is in fact wretched? Here is one origin story for our double lives. The first woman, having just been born from Adam's side, finds herself in a competitive conversation with a snake. "Can you really not eat any trees in the garden?" he asks. His exaggeration prompts an exaggerated reply: "We can eat *any* tree, but we can't even touch *that* one, lest we die." The snake then claims that God is not telling the truth – they will not die – and that God is jealous of them, not wanting them to become like gods. Suddenly the fruit looks delicious; Eve eats it and gives some to Adam.[6]

The outcome of eating the fruit for them is not becoming like a god as promised, but rather, developing a double life. They see their nakedness and cover it. They hide in the garden from God. Shame divides them from themselves and from God. Shame relative to what? one wonders. They feel shame relative to what they think they ought to be, to their divine pretenses. No god would have a tender, naked body. Perhaps the knowledge of good and evil promised by the fruit is real, but the evil turns out to be rooted in what is vulnerable and weak. Eternity is good; death is evil. To know this is to be torn by a double consciousness, unable not to long for eternity, unable to completely ignore my human nature, subject to ignorance, folly, death, and disease.

I admit to being a bit soft on the fall of humanity. As I see it, without this moment, without this divide in ourselves, we would not be who and what we are. Without competition and shame, we are too simple to be interesting.

Yet the fact remains that shame and doubleness are engines of human evil; they are wounds that must be healed if we are to be happy and good. Blessedly, after the Fall, our happiness and goodness need not make us less interesting, as the example of Francis of Assisi suggests all on its own. The task of redemption is to take up our competition and vanity as a part of the wholehearted pursuit of happiness with God. "Oh necessary sin of Adam!" is sung at the Easter vigil, and I feel it every time.

In the singleness of mind required for the right living, Christianity does not break with the ancient philosophers. Socrates models wholeheartedness, living in poverty, to the point of neglecting his family, for the sake of philosophy. Plato's masterpiece, the *Republic*, has as its central argument that justice is not merely the decoration of a successful life but is worth the sacrifice of success and every other good besides. Justice is worth everything. Aristotle famously counsels that we should not see our capacity for contemplative flourishing as limited by our human nature. As he exhorts us,

> We must not follow those who advise us, being men, to think of human things, and, being mortal, of mortal things, but must, so far as we can, make ourselves immortal, and strain every nerve to live in accordance with the best thing in us; for even if it be small in bulk, much more does it in power and worth surpass everything.[7]

The concern of the ancient philosophers, I think, was the fragility of lukewarmness, given the strength of our worst motives. We begin merely half-hearted in justice, enjoying our goodness and excellence alongside material success and political freedom, a say in our communities, luxury, and comfort. But as the later books of the *Republic* suggest, our half-hearted justice decays into hypocrisy. We hide secret wealth under our image of austere moderation, brutality under our respectable pursuit of wealth, childish or brutish indulgence under our sense of freedom.[8]

There is an irony for Christian followers of Plato and Aristotle. A central life-activity sought wholeheartedly – without compromise, for its own sake – is originally an aristocratic goal. Unlike manual laborers, whose work is for an external end, the philosopher finds his end within himself. Yet the central icon of Christian life is Christ, in Paul's words:

> who, though he was in the form of God
> did not deem equality with God something to be grasped at
> but he emptied himself, taking the form of a slave,
> being born in the likeness of human beings,
> and found in human form, he humbled himself
> becoming obedient unto death, even death on a cross.[9]

Followers of Christ do not strive for divinity. Rather, they humble themselves, deny themselves, and embrace the lives of slaves and sufferers. Both Aristotle and Paul have radical ideas of the highest good: There is such a thing, and it is worth everything. And yet the highest good for Paul seems to require not self-fulfilment or self-actualization but self-sacrifice.

In a way, the divide between Aristotle and Paul is perfectly logical. If we are divided, as Eve is, between awareness of our weakness and fragility and the desire to be godlike, we can find wholeheartedness in two ways: We can strive for divinity, like Aristotle, or embrace dependence, as Paul does. The choice would seem to rest on what the costs and benefits of striving for divinity really are, as compared with the costs and benefits of reconciling ourselves with our humanity under the eyes of a loving and personal God. Christian teaching, like classical philosophy, seeks to tame and shape our worst impulses, directing them, when possible, toward good. But unlike classical philosophy, it considers the desire for divinity as among our internal enemies.

If we take union with God in self-sacrificing love to be the highest end of a life, to constitute human happiness, what is required? Whether or not Paul suggests a shift in what we judge best, he certainly shifts our understanding of how we attain it. We do not "grasp" our highest end. Rather, we sacrifice it. In doing so, our happiness is bestowed on us as a prize: It is given, rather than taken. As the passage continues:

> On account of this God highly exalted him
> and gave him the name above every name,
> so that at the name of Jesus every knee might bend
> in heaven, on earth, and under the earth.[10]

The self-emptying of Christ described by Paul in Philippians plays a central role in religious life. The Dominican friars, for instance, take only one vow when they commit to their way of life: the vow of obedience. That obedience is meant to echo Christ's "obedience unto death, even death on a cross."

It is a sacrifice of one's will, one's capacity to choose, understood as the sacrifice Eve would not make. To vow obedience is to dedicate oneself to one thing with one's whole heart.

We may judge such renunciation admirable, or despicable, or pitiable – but how could it be recognizable as a form of happiness, or even a way to become happy? Yet the sacrifice of choice is not as alien to us as it sounds. We regularly live under the regime of other people's choices, and if we are lucky, we do so with our own consent. Certainly, when we choose to marry, or to have a child – that is, when we seek to love unconditionally – we make a choice to relinquish choosing. It is a form of surrender, or as I'll call it, abandonment. We may, just as lukewarm Christians do, imagine compromise – perhaps there can be a bit of what I want and a bit of what my child wants! – and even achieve it for a time. Our surrender may take a lifetime. But, if we are lucky, it will come.

At the end of the Gospel of John, the resurrected Jesus asks Peter three times if he loves him. With growing frustration, Peter answers, "Yes, yes, you know everything, you know that I love you." Jesus tells him to "feed his sheep," and gives the following warning:

> Amen, amen, I say to you, when you were younger, you used to dress yourself and go where you wanted; but when you grow old, you will stretch out your hands, and someone else will dress you and lead you where you do not want to go.[11]

Evidently, loving Jesus will be not be an active enterprise with its parts evaluated for effectiveness. On the contrary, it will be a surrender to the actions of others.

In Christianity, one's happiness is not within one's power, on principle. It must be given by grace. Part of the point of renunciation, then, is to clear the obstacles to grace: to break our habits of choosing that blind us to what we might receive. The contrast is not quite between getting and receiving, acting and suffering. Christian discipline involves the use of the will to choose to receive and to choose to suffer, habitually and freely and out of love.

The practice of total renunciation is an action, like the act of marriage, in which one holds one's whole life in view. The point is not to give up money for a time, to see what it is like, or to fast or wear a habit for a particular period of penance. It is an attempt to shape one's whole life. To examine it properly, then, we must think about the meaning of life, what makes a whole life valuable or worthwhile, what commitments are necessary to make our lives worth living. We will begin there in the next chapter.

1   The Call

> And all this comes to an end.
> And is not again to be met with.
> *Ezra Pound, "Exile's Letter" (after Rihaku)*

Mother Walatta Petros, an Ethiopian noblewoman of the seventeenth century, had four children in a row who died shortly after childbirth. After that, writes her hagiographer, she "bore in mind the transience of the world."[1] Her husband still loved her, but she no longer wanted to stay with him. She spent her days in prayer and fasting, and her nights in vigils. At holidays she threw banquets to which all were invited, the poor and the wretched along with the townspeople and the priests. When her husband left on a military campaign, she saw her chance. She gave away all her possessions, including all of her jewelry, "eighty ounces weight of gold," and with two monks and three servants walked all through the night.[2] They traveled several days to the monastic settlement at Zade, where Walatta Petros shaved her head, took a nun's cap, and swore to remain all her days.

Her husband, learning of her departure, was furious. His men destroyed the town near Zade and set out to arrest her. Seeing how much damage he was causing on her behalf, she returned to him. But her heart still sought the monastery. At the time, thanks to the arrival of European missionaries, the Roman Catholic faith had begun to make inroads into the ancient Christian practice of the Ethiopians. The king had adopted the "faith of the filthy Europeans" as the hagiographer calls it.[3] The Coptic Orthodox patriarch whom Walatta Petros followed had been murdered.

When Walatta Petros' husband showed sympathy with the Catholics, Walatta Petros stopped eating, drinking, and beautifying herself, and lived as a nun in her husband's household. Her husband finally let her go to live with her brother. From there she escaped again, only to be held captive by the king for a time, in an effort to make her renounce the Orthodox faith. At last, she was freed and able to pursue monastic life without interference. She continually gathered disciples, even while imprisoned. Once released, she moved frequently, forming all in all six communities; the last, for which she wrote a rule of life, was eight hundred strong.[4]

The vocation – the call to religious life – of Walatta Petros was rooted in a perception of the transience of things. Once she perceived it, she was moved to sacrifice married life, wealth, privilege, and beauty to follow Christ.

The grief of Walatta Petros and her call to religious life might be illuminated by a twentieth-century Orthodox nun who found her vocation after the death of her infant daughter. Mother Maria Skobtsova describes her manner of mourning:

> For [some] it is not even a question of grief, but the sudden opening of gates into eternity, while the whole of natural existence has lost its stability and its coherence, yesterday's laws have been abolished, desires have faded,

> meaninglessness has displaced meaning and a different, albeit incomprehensible Meaning has caused wings to sprout at one's back.... Into the grave's dark maw are plunged all hopes, plans, habits, calculations, and above all meaning, the whole meaning of life. In the face of this, everything needs to be reexamined or rejected against falsehood or corruption.

For Mother Maria Skobtsova, grief reveals the truth about the world:

> People call this a visitation of the Lord. A visitation which brings what? Grief? No, more than grief: for he suddenly reveals the nature of things.

Because grief brings us into contact with the nature of things – what Mother Walatta called "the transience of the world" – one can and ought to resist its fading and the return to the "normal" sense of things. Life without grief is "blindness":

> Eventually, they say, time heals – would it not be more accurate to say "deadens"? –all. Normality is gradually restored. The soul reverts to its blindness. The gates to eternity are closed once more ...
>
> And I am convinced that anyone who has shared this experience of eternity, if only once; who has understood which way he is going, if only once; who has perceived the One who precedes him, if only once: such a person will find it hard to deviate from this path, to him all comforts will appear ephemeral, all treasures valueless, all companions superfluous if in their midst he fails to see the one Companion, bearing his cross.[5]

For Mother Maria Skobtsova, the collapse of meaning in the heart of grief clarifies the eternal. The vision of death, since it destroys every illusion, reveals the reality that is beyond things that die.

———

In vocation stories, success is as common as grief in inspiring a disruptive discontent with ordinary life. In Teresa of Avila's account of the foundation of her monasteries, she tells the tale of another noblewoman with a religious vocation. Doña Casilda is beautiful and the heir to a large fortune. Her two older siblings have entered religious life themselves. Her relatives fear the same for her, so they betroth her to a relative when she is only ten or eleven years old. She falls deeply in love with her fiancé. Teresa writes:

> She had been spending a very happy day with her
> betrothed, whom she loved with an intensity rare for a
> child of her age, when suddenly she became very sad, for
> she realized that the day was over and that all other days
> would come to an end in the same way.[6]

She attends a liturgy where a young woman is clothed with the Carmelite habit. She is enchanted by the poverty of the monastery – one of Teresa's foundations – there, she thinks, one could really serve God. Visiting the convent later with her family, Doña Casilda asks the prioress to stay. Her family protests; the prioress refuses her request. She leaves the convent but begs to return. Her relatives insist that she is too young to enter religious life; she replies sharply that if she is old enough to marry (as they have insisted), she is old enough to give herself to God.

When staying with her grandmother, she asks to go into the country with her governess for some recreation, and arranges a gambit whereby they stop by the monastery to donate some wood and to ask for a jug of water. She slips inside and throws her arms around a statue of the Virgin Mary, begging the prioress to accept her. This time, the prioress agrees, and so her family has to remove her by royal order. Both her mother and her confessor oppose her, along with her relatives; she stays at her mother's house with her hostile family.

One day, attending Mass at a church with her mother and governess, her mother steps into the confessional. Doña Casilda acts quickly and sends her governess away to ask a priest for a Mass. In Teresa's account:

> She stuck her overshoes up her sleeves, caught up her skirt, and ran away with the greatest possible haste to this convent, which was a long way away.[7]

The governess tries and fails to overtake her; when she reaches the convent, they give her the habit at once.

The attraction to a vocation is strong enough to break all other human bonds, not only the bonds of romantic attachment but also the ties to one's parents and one's origins. In her novel about the nineteenth-century French missionaries to the American Southwest, *Death Comes for the Archbishop*, Willa Cather describes two young curates who promise an American bishop to join his missions, without telling their parents.[8] The two friends meet at dawn in secret to catch the coach to Paris, where they will be trained and sent out. One of them, his father a widower, has been walking the fields all night, his face swollen with tears. His friend takes his arm and reminds him that he can be absolved of his promise to the Ohio bishop, once he gets to Paris. In the end they both cross the ocean, without saying goodbye to their families, and die in the land of their missions.

Thomas Aquinas, too, fought for his vocation. His noble parents intended him to become the abbot of a wealthy monastery. While studying in Naples, Thomas met the new radical community of the Dominicans, who renounced land and wealth to serve as itinerant preachers, begging for their necessities. He joined them. In response, his family kidnapped Thomas en route to the Dominican community in Paris and kept him in captivity for a year. While Thomas was confined, his brothers sent a courtesan to him in the hopes that he would be seduced from his vocation. With the help of two angels, he chased her from the room with a torch. He escaped his parents – according to some accounts, lowered from a window on a rope – and made his life with the Dominicans.[9]

It is impossible to believe that a bloodless intellectual conviction could motivate such determined sacrifices. Nor could ambition, at least not obviously. These particular men and women sacrifice all of the benefits of wealth and nobility, not only comfort, but prestige and power, the typical objects of human striving. What drives these men and women? What shapes their determination?

Certainly, fear can drive a person to extremes – think of Maria of *The Sound of Music* (1965), who flees back to her convent once she realizes she is in love with her employer. But

Maria's fear is not strong enough to hold out against the kind advice of the superior to return. In what becomes a repeated refrain in popular films of religious life: to be drawn to religion isn't a losing or a fleeing, but a finding and a seeking.[10] It is possible that some have sufficient fear of life in the world to drive them to religious life. Still, it seems worthwhile to test the hypothesis that fits the phenomena more closely: These are men and women in love.

In love with what or whom? With poverty perhaps – we will return to that possibility. Or like Antony, Martin, and Francis, they are in love with the Jesus Christ of the Gospels, the Poor Man of poor men. Yet I would like to begin with the problem that sets the background for the passion's development. Mother Walatta feels the transience of things; Doña Casilda notices that even the best days come to an end. Such insights could inspire resignation, depression, or despair, but they do not. These women are in love, I suggest, with God as transcendent and eternal. That love is sparked by an insight that leads them to reject the ordinary objects of love: wealth, power, and even distinctive human individuals, husband, fiancé, mother, father.

All Is Vanity

What is the insight that provokes Doña Casilda to give up her beloved? She realizes after a wonderful day that it will end like all the others. She sees a life dedicated to romantic love and marriage as futile. Romantic love, in our North American and European culture, is the pinnacle of a human life. The young teen longs for it; the elderly pine its loss; in between is the drama of marriage, bereavement, divorce, adultery, friendship, and loneliness.

The futility of even a life infused with a happy romance is taken up with unusual clarity in the 2013 Polish film *Ida*. Ida was left on the door of a convent as an infant during the Second World War and raised by the nuns. When she is preparing to make her profession and join the community, her superior tells her that her family is Jewish. Before taking her vows, she is told, she must meet her only surviving relative. She leaves the convent for the first time and gets to know her aunt Wanda, a famously brutal prosecutor for the Soviet-sponsored government. She also meets an attractive young musician. She returns to the convent, disquieted, and postpones her vows.

In her time away from the convent, Ida, like Walatta Petros, has had an encounter with death. She and her aunt, in their time together, have learnt about the murder of Ida's parents and Wanda's young son, and have transferred their remains to a Jewish cemetery. In their travels, it becomes evident that Wanda assuages her pain with casual sex and heavy drinking. These medications fail in the long term. After Ida returns to the convent, Wanda commits suicide.

Ida leaves the convent again for the funeral, where the musician seeks her out. They spend the night together. The next morning, he invites her to spend the day with his band. "And after that?" she asks. "We buy a dog." "And after that?" "We get married, have a few kids." She asks, "And after that?" He answers, "The usual. Life." She recognizes this answer as an evasion of an unanswerable question. She puts her habit back on and walks back to the convent.

"This day will end like all others." "And after that?" Both of these women inquire into the meaning of life and encounter the transience of things. It seems to them that since even the most wonderful experiences happen in a sequence, one after another, each coming to an end, they cannot qualify as goods that make life worth living. All of the goods a person might dream of or strive for, including the most meaning-laden activities and experiences, turn to dust.

Why does a recognition of the transience of things make life in the world seem pointless? Death is as old as Adam, yet human endeavor continues as if it makes no difference. If we find ourselves in crises of meaning, we can live in the moment, taking each day as it comes. Can we not "kiss a joy as it flies," as Blake put it – treasure our loves and our work for what they are in the moment?

Could living in the moment console Walatta Petros for her lost children? The answer must be no. No matter how real and concrete the joy at the birth of a new human being into the world, the grief of his or her lost future would swallow it right up. To try to see it otherwise stretches human capacities to the point of cruelty. "Live in the moment" is common advice, containing real wisdom, but on its face, it assumes a certain prosperity. It is quite difficult to follow such advice when our moments are laden with grief or disfigured by deprivation – at least, unless we find a way to value grief and deprivation themselves. As I discuss further on, grief and deprivation can be treasured in the state of Christian abandonment, as a union with Christ crucified. Only there, I think, can "live in the moment" be sound advice.

The story of Doña Casilda illustrates that the recognition of the transience of things belongs to joy as well as grief, to success as well as failure. The brilliant poet of transience, author of the book of Ecclesiastes, writes in the voice of King Solomon:

> A generation goes and a generation comes, but the earth remains forever ... What there was, that will be; what was done, that will be done, but there is nothing new under the sun.[11]

Grand palaces and gardens, fine wine and beautiful women, all amount to nothing. Even wisdom – the gift for which Solomon is most renowned – is pointless, since the wise man and the fool go to the same place, the grave.[12]

Ecclesiastes speaks to the emptiness of all things from the perspective of the wealthiest, wisest, and most powerful king of Israel, and his words are echoed nowhere more closely than in the speeches of Job, the once wealthy man who loses his property along with his twelve children in a single day.[13] Job sits scratching his boils with a potsherd, scolded and belittled by his comforters, demanding that God justify his fate. Solomon, in his cushy palace surrounded by every luxury, does not demand or lament as Job does. But his success yields insight similar to that yielded by Job's grief.

What insights do these two ancient wise men share? For one: Death makes all acquisition futile; it reduces us to the poverty of birth:

> As [the rich man] came forth from his mother's womb, so again shall he depart, naked as he came, having nothing from his labor that he can carry in his hand.[14]

To seek justice or practice mercy is pointless: it does not guarantee flourishing, which more often goes to the wicked: "Why do the wicked survive, grow old, become mighty in power?"[15] Both the justice of the just man and the wickedness of the wicked man are annihilated in death.

> As it is for the good man, so it is for the sinner; as it is for him who swears rashly, so it is for him who fears an oath. Among all the things that happen under the sun, this is the worst, that things turn out the same for all.[16]

To both authors, God is defined by absolute power and total obscurity. His plans are secret, and his omnipotent will cannot be overturned – what God does cannot be undone by any human endeavor. "Whatever God has done will endure forever; there is no adding to it, or taking away from it. Thus has God done, that he may be revered."[17] Despite God's universal and implacable governance, his work is impossible to understand: "Just as you know not how the breath of life fashions the human frame in the mother's womb, so you know not the work of God, which he is accomplishing in the universe."[18] All in all, it is best not to be born. The grief caused by seeing the futility and vanity of human life is not worth anything.[19]

It is Solomon, not Job, who promotes enjoyment of the good things in life, life in the moment. Of course! The king is the one who has them. The savoring of the moment is, it seems, for the lucky – not for everyone.

If you, like me, are an emotionally volatile lover of literature, you cannot read poetry as beautiful as Solomon's or Job's and not believe, somehow, that what they say must be true. But such sentimentality does not befit philosophers. Is it true that the transience of things, the inevitability of death and of endings, drains ordinary life of its value? The philosopher Thomas Nagel famously argues that it does not.[20] Nagel argues that if something matters, no extension of the duration of its existence makes it matter more, any more than its small size, expanded, would also increase the degree it matters. For Nagel, it is our unlimited capacity to seek justification, not the structure of our desires, that forces absurdity. Life seems pointless and absurd only because we are always able to question any candidate for its meaning.

Nagel has mis-framed the problem and come to a solution too easily. When we seek a meaningful life, we mean a satisfying life, a life that is worth the trouble. I can formulate a question in words that has no impact on my general sense of satisfaction. Life is pointless and absurd not because we can always seek a further justification, but only when we deeply care about things we cannot have. The absurdity that matters is when our passion for the unattainable drives us to approach life with the wrong tools, like emptying a lake with a sieve. Whether this is true can only be settled by looking at what human beings care deeply about, asking if they can have it, and, if not, how the desire for it might be managed.

Nagel's claim that the universal destiny of destruction does not strip life of meaning relies on thinking that something's duration does not affect whether it matters or not. If it matters now, it will not matter more for lasting for longer; if it doesn't matter, no length of time will grant it the power to do so. Nagel has assumed value and added time. He has not considered that time or how we imagine time plays a significant, even a necessary role, in giving things value.

Loving something entails wanting it to last.[21] That is so for a beloved human being as much as it is for a treasured teapot. Some precious experiences are essentially shaped by having an ending, like a piece of music or a particular conversation. But if a beloved piece of music or a conversation partner were to be permanently extinguished from the face of the earth, our response would be grief.[22]

It is true that our experiences are episodic, but it is also true that we carefully cultivate the objects of our experience, taking care of or supporting them (if they are people), donating or volunteering to support them (if they are experiences), preserving and developing them (if they are lands, places, communities, or objects). These are the activities that seem to give human life on earth its meaning. We also create and invent, seeking new experiences or the recovery of old ones. But we could not do any of this unless we imagine what we build or nurture will last.[23] As we live our lives, caring for people, music, dance, conversation, or other endeavors, we don't simply add experiences together. We perceive greater and greater richness in their objects, caring about them and dreading their loss all the more with the passage of time.

How long do we want what we love to last? The fact that we are often reconciled to the chaotic destruction and replacement of various beloved things does not mean that we desire them to last only a certain time. When we are truly reconciled to the loss of something, it is because we have found something new, put our focus elsewhere, when our love has effectively died. We divide our attention, hedging our bets against grief and loss. We love conditionally; when the conditions fail, our love fails, and we move onto something else. But I reckon that to hold something in loving attention while reconciled to its permanent annihilation is not humanly possible. If it does not seem this way, it is because we have found substitute forms of survival – a stone grave marker, a memory, an album of photographs, a memorial project, a young person with the name or the voice of the dead – that continue.

The fear of death and the fear of loss then, may be one ground of our automatic half-heartedness, our difficulties in devoting ourselves to something completely. Wholeheartedness means putting all our eggs in one basket and waiting for them to break – as all eggs surely will. Lukewarmness is the natural condition of self-protection against loss. Philosopher Eleonore Stump calls it "willed loneliness."[24]

It is true that experiences and relationships would lose their poignancy if we did not die.[25] But it is also true that they would not be poignant at all if we did not long for them to last, even unto the end of time. Poignancy results from a clash between a desire and the nature of its object. We seek eternity and get poignancy. To treasure poignancy above eternity is to treasure the terms of our dissatisfaction. So we face the central question to which Christian teaching responds: Is there anything that can satisfy our desire for a joy outside of time?

———

For Mother Walatta Petros, it is the deaths of her children that spark the insight into the transience of things. How much of our life or work is about our children? Consider a world without children, as portrayed in the 2006 film of P. D. James' novel, *Children of Men*, directed by Alfonso Cuarón.[26] In the film, every human on earth was suddenly stricken infertile twenty years earlier. The youngest person on earth is twenty-one years old. The schoolyards are empty, and endemic violence is narrated by a competing array of propaganda machines. Only fanatics seem to have projects of any scope. Life under these circumstances appears utterly pointless.[27]

The threat the scenario poses is not to the childless, but to any of us. The lives of childless persons like myself have meaning thanks to other people's children. I am a teacher. I pass on to young people the habits of mind I learned myself when I was young. They shall (I hope) replace me as teachers of the young when I am no more. If there are no young people, there is nothing and no one to teach; those habits of mine will die with me and my contemporaries. So too with any endeavor: starting a company, planting a farm, building a skyscraper, lobbying for justice. These are instrumental endeavors, of course: The company makes possible leisure time with my family; the farm permits a rural life; lobbying for justice makes it possible for others to live fuller lives, packed with meaning. Either way, without the people of the future, what could any of this mean? It appears to be all reduced to momentary entertainment.

The scenario of the film raises the broader prospect that the meaning of our activities is a sort of optical illusion.

After all, should we imagine that the last generation of fertile humans *did have* a meaningful life?[28] Is the last round of childbearing rendered meaningless by the catastrophe that follows it? Perhaps one generation is not enough to make the previous one valuable. How about the one before that? How many generations are sufficient to generate lives of value and meaning? If we know that the human race will come to an end – and surely it will – why should anything at all matter?

The Swedish vessel, the Vasa, built in the early seventeenth century, was among the grandest ever made, decorated with hundreds of brightly colored wooden sculptures and armed with enormous brass cannons. It was launched with great fanfare into the Stockholm harbor in 1628. It sank from the force of two gusts of wind, 390 feet from shore. Its hull was pulled out in 1961 and sits in a Stockholm museum, a monument to the futility of human endeavor.

What is the difference between a great ship that sinks after five minutes and one that sinks after some days? What if it lasts for some years? A ship's value can be weighed against the profits it brings, which emerge over time; voyage after voyage, it begins to pay off the costs of building it, and to exceed them. It might break even in one voyage, or twenty. But we are not weighing materials against materials, but the value of a life, or several lives. How much is a human lifespan worth – human desire, enterprise, endeavor, accomplishment?

Consider the tragedy of the work of ten years, or a lifetime, undone before one's eyes. One dedicates one's life to a company (for an easier life), a school or a philosophy department (to cultivate minds), a church (to nurture souls), a small business (to serve a community), any institution or enterprise. When we are too advanced in years to begin again, it crumbles as we watch, along with the human activities our endeavors made possible. Our work has been futile. Now imagine that the crumbling takes place just after our death. Our work is still futile. Yet, we know, everything crumbles. We have most of us walked in the ruins of empires. Nothing lasts forever. Why not draw the conclusion that all our endeavor is futile?

Of course, we have experiences that feel complete in themselves: the walk in the woods, the symphony, the dance, late-night conversations with friends that continually lapse into laughter, holding your infant in your arms and looking at its tiny fingernails. These experiences may hold ultimate value, existential value, in a way that building things over years does not. Yet, again, we build things over years to secure those experiences. We cultivate things for the sake of something of more fundamental value, yes; but those riches of life in which life culminates also depend on their continuous cultivation. That is why the work of building is so meaningful and so gratifying, and why its undoing is so painful.

The problem we have been circling around is worse than facing one's own death. Death can be borne, I think, if one knows that the things and people one cares about live on afterward. What we are looking at is annihilation, the destruction of everything. I am persuaded that if death alone does not render life meaningless, annihilation certainly does.

Eternity in the Heart

Solomon describes the futility of human endeavor as a work of God. God has given everything its proper time and season, birth, death, planting, sowing, grief, joy. "He has made each thing beautiful in its time."[29] The promise of wisdom is that the wise person comes to know these times and seasons.[30] However, even the wisest of us is ignorant of what is to come, and none of us is master of our life or death. Solomon diagnoses our resulting discomfort:

> [God] also put the world [or: eternity] into their hearts, so that man cannot find out the work of God from beginning to end.[31]

We might have been put together in such a way as to enjoy the world simply as it is presented to us, taking in each thing, beautiful at its proper time, accepting our end as it comes, unforeseen. But we are not. God has put the world into our hearts. We long to see the future unfold indefinitely. We want to know everything and to act in such a way as to make a permanent mark. Just as we seek to know what is always and universally true, we seek to act under the aspect of eternity, to build monuments that will last forever.

In the countries where I have lived, the resting places of the dead are marked with carved stone. The stones are meant to last, it seems, as long as the inscriptions of the Assyrian kings. But our graves will stop mattering within a few generations. We may be charmed by an ancient cenotaph, but chances are, its living relations have long ago forgotten it. Our desire for things to last may not be fully rational or easily guided by the fact of the matter. We imagine that things go on and on. But they do not. Everything dies, is destroyed, or falls out of range of human attention, losing its meaning.

Our desire for eternity need not be conscious. Could we act, could we do anything at all, if we had a vivid sense of the lifespan of its results? When we have the privilege of calculating costs and benefits, of course we can: We can build a furnace that will last a hundred years and longer, paying for its materials and more. The film *Arrival* (2016) hypothesizes that we would choose to have a child, knowing that it would live only ten years. It invites a cruel question: would we so choose, if we knew it would live but five years? One year? A single breath?

What would we be like if we had no sense of indefinite time, of lasting forever, or if we had no sense of the whole of time or space? Yet the desires provoked by global imaginings cannot be satisfied. "The eye is not satisfied with seeing, nor the ear with hearing."[32] We are small in width and stature, we are blind to the future, and we die.

Either a lawnmower works, or it doesn't. Machines don't lie. But a human life can run in circles and insist that those circles are proper functioning. Religious life and all of its renunciations begin from the recognition of our broken machinery and reach with all human power for the work that gives our lives meaning and that fulfills our deepest desires.

The desire for eternity is not straightforward or transparent. It hides underneath our more ordinary loves and desires. The ambition to change the world is not only limited by the ravages of time but is actually fed by illusions.

The "world" we can reshape is nothing like the whole that lies only in our heart, known only by love. We reduce the world to a given sphere – say, academic philosophy; the small town we live in; the actions and passions of a handful of political figures, whose actions seem rather less deliberate and less effective than those of an ordinary carpenter. When we exhaust ourselves in burnout and in midlife crises, we turn to crafts: gardening, woodwork, knitting. Here at least our action is effective, even if our scope is much more limited.

It isn't only our goals that are futile. It is also our leisurely activity. Time may drop away in a spirited card game or in the silence of nature, boating down a cliff-bordered river among the diving kingfishers. We may think or study without any end in view – for as long as we have, our understanding grows, and is worth whatever time is spent. It is the very timelessness of these activities that puts the world into our hearts, to make us long for joy that never ends. Such activities cannot be properly added up into a sum of accomplishments, any more than a single minute of excruciating pain could be traded for an equivalent number of minutes of a pain proportionately less.[33] We cannot help wanting eternity – not everlasting activity where our muscles get sore, our eyes tired, and our souls sink into boredom – but a joy that does not end, just as our best activities tantalizingly suggest.

If our activities are sometimes directed at accomplishment, other times on experiences holding their value in themselves, in which sense does our longing for immortality lie? Allow me to speculate. Accomplishment is a means of power over our circumstances, a way of evading fragility and vulnerability. Eve's desire to be a god – as much as my own busy effort to endeavor, control, or manage – is an anxious response to inevitable decay and destruction. That can be so even if my intention is not direct. My pleasure in weeding, or hunting, may well lie in my exercising power over my surroundings, the setting of my strength against that of something else, and winning. This is not so much an evasion of death as an evasion of the condition for death: weakness, powerlessness, hapless receptivity to circumstances.

A project may be completed successfully or not, but its completion always fails to make us invincible. Likewise, the coming-to-an-end of a treasured activity, or the death or collapse of the thing we loved in it, proves that we have not escaped time at all. Not only will that activity, once restarted, again come to an end, but the beloved objects and companions in that activity, the friends, family members, cliff-lined river, also will all come to an end.

Perhaps indestructible knowledge alone can satisfy my deepest longings. Even so, as Solomon understood about wisdom, what matters to me is *my* knowing, and that dies with me, as in the famous description of the death of the Homeric warrior "who lay in a whirl of dust ... having forgotten horsemanship."[34]

Myself and Others

If this sort of argument undermines the consolations of our collective future, what possibilities remain for understanding the value of a single human life? When I first began teaching philosophy, I had my students read a paper by utilitarian philosopher Jonathan Glover called "The Sanctity of Life."[35]

Glover argues against the idea of the sanctity of life by claiming that since we would choose death over permanent unconsciousness and over continuous terrible pain, neither life nor consciousness matter in themselves. For Glover, lives are only valuable when they are worth living. In one class, I tried again and again to explain the argument, but the classroom, full of Alabama Christians, could not catch on. Finally, I said: "He's asking what value your life has for you!" and a young woman asked, "Why would you think that the value of your life was for *you*?" My jaw hit the floor. I had never heard such a thing.

The only thing that has equal value to a human life, absent God, is another human life. That is the insight behind our commonplace wisdom that love is all we need, or that lives of service, teaching, nursing, search and rescue, farming and food service, parenting, the administration of justice, the care of the poor, the defense of the innocent, are the truly meaningful lives. So Mother Maria Sbotsova reflects, after the death of her daughter:

> For years I did not know, in fact I never knew the meaning of repentance, but now I am aghast at my own insignificance. At Nastia's side I feel that my soul has meandered down back alleys all my life. And now I want an authentic and purified road, not out of faith in life, but in order to justify, understand, and accept death. No amount of thought will ever result with any greater formulation than the three words, "Love one another", so long as it is love to the end and without exceptions. And then the whole of life is illumined, which is otherwise an abomination and a burden.[36]

Mother Maria, in the face of the death of her child, sees all human endeavor as useless, swallowed up by annihilation. At that point, she felt, she had no alternative but to respond, by dedicating her life to love of her neighbors. This she did, until her attempts to hide and protect the Jews of Paris got her sent to Ravensbruck and murdered by the Nazis. Yet I doubt she thought her work would be rendered futile by such an end. She has found in the love of her neighbors that "the whole of life is illumined." That suggests that something eternal and transcendent is found there, something that lies behind everything we experience.

———————

I have had, more or less, a sheltered and comfortable life. The time just before my conversion was a remarkably happy one. I had found moderate success in a high-prestige graduate program; I was able to relax enough to feel that I had been accepted not as an aspiring phony, but as myself. Yet it was suddenly and violently exposed to me that I was living in radical contingency and world-cracking suffering.

My exposure to this reality took place as I witnessed the transformation of the World Trade Center into smoke, ash, and human remains, all in minutes. I watched the news coverage on live television, in a student common room on the campus where I was studying at the time. I sat with one of my teachers, among the most self-assured, implacable people I had ever met. He kept turning to me and asking, like a child, "The buildings are gone?," "They're really gone?," "Are they not there anymore?," "I can't believe those buildings aren't there anymore."

The towers of the old World Trade Center were enormous. One saw them from outside the city, from a long way off, in the car or on the train traveling in. Once, visiting the city with friends, we took the elevator to the top of one of the towers. Through vast windows, we saw a thunderstorm, well below us, flashing lightning as it moved across the city, from Brooklyn into lower Manhattan. I had never been above a thunderstorm, before – or since. It was magnificent to see something that would be overwhelming or dangerous on the ground reduced to a beautiful entertainment, harmless as a school of tropical fish.

It came out on the news that day that a task force on the earlier bombing of the World Trade Center had recommended a terrorism response center. It had been planned, built, staffed, and located . . . in the World Trade Center. The managed safety of the wealthy and the powerful was in the rubble, just as the rescue teams, fire, police, the helpers, were themselves rubble. The civic effort of one of the richest cities in the world to preserve life and prevent catastrophe had failed.

The bombing shook my privileged sense of the safety and predictability of the world into shambles. Anything could happen; I gobbled rumors, speculations, deeply unnerved by the vast new landscape of possible events and experiences that opened up. An evening thunderstorm sounded like a bombing raid; a rumor of a threat resonated in waves of fear.

No one I knew died in the bombing. Yet I was not only overwhelmed with a sense of contingency and fear, that the whole world could change in a matter of minutes, but with grief. I lived an hour away from the city. At the local rail station, homemade flyers with pictures of missing loved ones were stuck up with tape. I wept daily over the newspaper, which published story after story of bereaved spouses, grieving parents, and orphaned children, alongside the acts of heroism that emerged, slowly, from the rubble. All in a moment, daily life, its tedium, its joys, its frustrations, had evaporated, and a new dimension of value, a different level of love and self-sacrifice, had opened up. On the one hand, life had been emptied of its previous meaning, as Mother Maria Sbotsova described. On the other, "the whole of life had been illumined" – something shone out that I had not seen previously.

We began by asking what drove Mother Walatta Petros, Doña Casilda, and many others to renounce wealth, rank, power, romantic love, and filial duty to serve God alone. The perception of the futility or transience of things did not provoke despair or resignation: It was the occasion for falling in love. But that object of love still evades us. Whatever it is that motivates these tremendous actions of courage and endurance, we know at this point only its basic shape: the shape suggested by Solomon, the shape of the eternal, the timeless, and the complete. It is the shape of God himself that he has put into our hearts. As another courageous renunciant put it: "Our hearts are restless until they rest in thee."[37]

2 Blessed Are the Poor

We began in the last chapter with a puzzle about how men and women with everything, wealth, position, good looks, and love – would leave everything for an austere life dedicated to God. I have suggested that it is the eternal, timeless, transcendent God that appears to fill the gaping hole left when our deepest desires encounter the world. This may be true enough, but it is very incomplete. The philosophical vocations of the Hellenistic and Roman eras also sought out eternity and transcendence. Yet their stories have quite a different flavor. One might seek tranquility in the face of inevitable death, as the Epicureans did; or unity with a cosmic source of wisdom, as the Stoics did; or a prophetic rejection of human pretense, as Diogenes the Cynic did. The Christian God is transcendent, but also lives intimately with us. Intimacy with a transcendent and timeless God is a difficult thing to understand or to articulate. Yet we must try, since the religious we have described are evidently acting on a passionate, personal love, as befits a personal God.

The shock of contingency comes through serious illness, the collapse of a treasured institution, an encounter with death, a sudden grief. Once the realm of suffering is seen, it is difficult not to see. As Mother Maria Skobtsova put it: "Into the grave's dark maw are plunged all hopes, plans, habits, calculations, and above all meaning, the whole meaning of life." To one who has seen what she calls "eternity" in this way:

to him all comforts will appear ephemeral, all treasures valueless, all companions superfluous if in their midst he fails to see the one Companion, bearing his cross.[1]

It is a Poor Man, the Christ who "emptied himself, taking the form of a slave" whom they imitate and who offers a transfigured mode of being to them. The Poor Man and his poverty are the objects of their passionate desire.

For our examples thus far, poverty is the central matter in view. It is the poverty of Teresa's convent that strikes Doña Casilda after her realization that romance will not provide meaning to her life. Mother Walatta's gold is the first thing to go when she leaves her palace. It is the wealth of the Benedictines that drives Thomas Aquinas to the poor beggars, the Dominicans. Poverty draws both Francis and Antony from their wealth, and poverty melts the heart of Martin of Tours in his life as a Roman conscript.

As it stands, the link between catastrophe, poverty, and love, is mysterious. I suggest in what follows two aspects of the attraction of poverty: living in truth and the encounter with a loving God. These two fundamental elements of Christian spiritual life are not unique to poverty; we will meet them again when we look at other ascetic practices, such as silence, solitude, community life, obedience, and celibacy.

Living in Truth

One need not grow up in poverty to view it with fear, shame, and intense aversion. My grandparents on both sides were professionals, doctors and engineers, descended from other doctors and engineers. My parents were middle-class in culture and background but lived well below their origins in the time of my childhood, drawn by a kind of downward mobility. My father worked in local childcare centers and lived by choice in the poorest neighborhood in San Francisco. My mother was a single mom, taking odd secretarial jobs and free-lance work. In my early childhood we took government assistance; I wore hand-me-downs from my brother up until middle school.

We lived in the borderlands between the middle class on one side and, on the other, families and communities that were ravaged by drugs, crime, incarceration, abuse, and other forms of violence and precarity. Those borderlands were barely metaphorical. My mother lived in a ramshackle Victorian in a gentrifying neighborhood; my father lived in a government-subsized highrise. We regularly visited the beautiful suburban homes of our grandparents. I alternated between private schools, where I was marked by poverty, and public ones, where I was marked by snobbery. I resisted the pressure downward, which alienated me from my working-class peers, but I bore sufficient marks of lower rank to alienate me from the solid middle-classers as well. I belonged nowhere, enveloped as I was by seemingly insurmountable social awkwardness. I wanted more than anything to lose the sense of shame I felt from both directions.

It was shame at the shadow of poverty and the ambition to escape it that drove me as far from my native territory as I could manage, attending college across the country in the comfort and prestige of a colonial-era redbrick liberal arts college, and going yet further east across the Atlantic to begin graduate school. At last, in my late twenties, I found myself where I wanted to be; I was a graduate student in one of the richest universities in the world, marked by its absurdly clean replicas of medieval Gothic buildings. I was surrounded by brilliant, interesting, respectable people, and able to relax in confidence that I could stay in such an environment if I so chose.

Like many academics, I chose academic life because I wanted a life that was more dignified, safer and more secure, more beautiful, more loving, in which I was more affirmed, appreciated, and understood, by contrast with the life I had come from. Like many aspirers – or in the derogatory term, social climbers – my rough edges stood out at first. But I made my way, aided by good looks, talent, charm, and, not least, my total concentration on my task of advancement.

Our aspirations are not only for goods like comfort or esteem. We aspire, like Eve, to free ourselves from the shame of weakness, vulnerability, contingency, and death. We want to be our own gods, in control of our destinies. Our desires for better lives are natural, rational, and good; but the aspiration for divine authority hides behind them. Our divine pretenses fuel the better parts of ourselves, like a hidden flame. We begin to imagine that somehow our success is thanks to our own efforts, and our own just reward, rather than relying on a thousand lucky contingencies. The truth about who we are and what truly belongs to us only unearths itself in a crisis, or through deliberate ascetic practice.

In 2001, as I have mentioned, I caught sight of the realm of contingency, catastrophe, and the realm of human suffering, and it began to reveal its heights and depths. From where I was, a successful graduate student at an extremely wealthy university, a training ground for the world's leaders, I now belonged to the "helping" class, the class that fixed things. So the obvious response to the crisis was through conventional forms of leadership: policy making, human rights work, the intelligence services. In the wake of the bombings, I turned to these areas with zealous interest. I went to hear lectures and panels with experts of various kinds. I read foreign-policy journals and sat in on classes on international peacemaking. I looked for a place for myself in these professional endeavors.

After some months, I realized, albeit only at the level of instinct, that these professions would not answer the sort of desire that now burned in me. I could not understand why. In retrospect, I think I reacted to the high altitude of the professions, their seat on a platform of power and prestige far above the people they meant to help. I recall during this time going to a one-day conference on the slave trade in the Sudan. The philosophers and economists considered the question of whether ransoming the enslaved caused more slavery. The discussion was shown toward the end to rely on a false assumption, one we had made in our ignorance of the real-life situation we had intended to discuss. We took a break for lunch: filet mignon with roasted vegetables, fresh berries and fine pastry. The suffering of the world was diminished to entertainment for a high-end social gathering.

I resolved to stay for the time being in academic life, despite my puzzlement as to how to reconcile it with the wound in my heart that had opened up.[2] I finished my degree and began teaching, and shortly thereafter entered the Church. I moved to Baltimore and found myself constantly confronted by the hidden destitution of the United States. I drove through neighborhoods without power, occupied by squatters, with boarded up windows and broken glass in the streets. Unlike most American cities, poverty there could not be avoided; if one just leaned toward not avoiding it, it came before the eyes and ears constantly.

As my vision improved, I became increasingly exhausted by my own selfishness. The speaking invitation, the job offer, the publication, the compliment, the successful paper, or the display of intellectual virtuosity all began to lose their kick. Addicts report seeking again and again the same reward from the same drug, even as it deadens and becomes hollow. I was in this sense very much like an addict to signs of my competitive success.

To begin to remedy my situation, I tacked on various types of volunteer work to my full-time teaching and my academic research. I began with literacy tutoring and hospice work; then I tried out a refugee resettlement center, a soup kitchen, and a shelter for pregnant women. There I found the limits of my imagined godlike powers to create or to heal. As a hospice volunteer, at the bedside of a woman dying of pancreatic cancer, learning and intelligence were useless. Mere humanity – to perceive, to stand still, to sympathize in silence, to offer a small kindness – was everything.

I developed a distinct longing *not* to make a difference. I was attracted to the poor and to poverty, but I had realized some of the nearby hazards. If I wished to witness a rags-to-riches story in which I played a central role, I was playing God, wallowing in self-importance, and diminishing the poor whom I pretended to serve. They would become puppets in a show where I was always the star.

I realized that the harder the service, the more wholesome it would be for me. I wanted to receive nothing from my activities other than the knowledge that I loved others and depended on God. I had to mortify my consolations: my sense of importance and my sense of righteousness, along with praise, approval, and status.

The Catholic practice of mortification has a dreary reputation. We are to put to death our attachments, to strip ourselves of them until we are naked. In fact, mortification is a straightforward form of self-examination and training in rational desire. If I am paid handsomely for my philosophical inquiries – in money, status, the impact of my name on a stranger in an airplane, sexual favors from the person of my choosing, or recognition and consideration – then I do not know why I pursue philosophy. I may think that I am pursuing the truth or the intellectual good of my fellow human beings, but I may be lying to myself. The proof is in the pudding: What would I do if the rewards were stripped away?

If my motives are mixed, and I would like to seek wholeheartedly what is best, to desire the right things in the right way for the right reasons, I can take steps to unmix my motives by taking away the rewards the bad motives seek.

Without their sought satisfactions, the bad motives at worst would be noisy and ineffective; at best, over time, their power might slowly diminish. I might mortify my consolations as a temporary measure as an inquiry into my motives, or in a permanent attempt to shape them. Either way, the suffering of it is not sought as such. The point is to find clarity of thought and to instill wholeheartedness.

Mortification is training in love. If I always grab the biggest cookie from the platter by instinct, it is possible I will not harm anyone on a given occasion. Perhaps the other cookie-eaters prefer less cookie or are watching their diet. But if my habit is set in this way, I run the risk that I will miss the time when the biggest cookie ought to go to others– for instance, if there is someone present who has spent the night in tears, someone who is unusually hungry, or someone who hasn't eaten a cookie in ten years. I can't be sure when that moment will come. So I train myself to take the smallest cookie, or no cookie at all, so that I can be sure that I can do the loving thing when opportunity arises, when I have no time to develop a new habit. It has nothing to do with guilt or with the hatred of one's own enjoyment. Indeed, my delight in cookies will be honed and intensified if I restrain myself from eating them at every impulse.

To mortify my love of the poor, to strip the consolations from it, I had to set out for the darkest places. Which, in the United States, meant going to jail. At a gathering of local Catholic charities, I heard a woman talk about her experiences in a prison ministry. She spoke with particular fervor about the inmates themselves, at how much she had learned from listening to them.

The poor are sent to jail in the USA on the slightest pretext, and getting out again, even when innocent beyond doubt, can be very challenging. But going to jail as a middle-class volunteer is very difficult. I filed multiple applications multiple times; I called numbers and sent emails that no one answered. Finally admitted to a volunteer orientation, I found ministers who viewed the inmates as hapless sinners, well beneath the volunteers. It seemed their care for them was offered conditionally, if the inmates played their appointed parts in a prefabricated drama of redemption. I walked away. At last, more than a year later, I was able to connect with a Sister of St. Joseph, the chaplain at the local women's jail. With her help, I set up a Bible study for women who were interested. I recruited another volunteer with an ad in the church bulletin, and for many months, the two of us went in, every other Saturday. I've never been in a darker place.

The jail had been closed by federal court order twenty years previously and had remained open on stays and exemptions ever since. (It did close, at long last, in 2019). The jail was a maze of tiled and windowless hallways, lit by fluorescent lights. A stomach-turning smell wafted from the cafeteria. The women slept in dormitories, thirty to a room, some addicts in withdrawal, some mentally ill, some sleepless for ordinary reasons. The chaplain supplied clothes and basic toiletries from her own resources. The activity room where we held our studies had a hole in the ceiling, right in its center, where rainwater poured through into a large trash can. When it really poured rain, my partner and I discovered, the sewers overflowed outside, and one could not leave or enter the jail without traversing a literal river of sewage, six to eight inches deep. These overflows happened often enough that the jail officers kept hip boots; one officer told me the sewers had overflowed regularly for at least twenty-five years.

The women who came to the Bible study were in circumstances far removed from any I had lived. They often had only the clothes on their backs. They came to our meetings seeking consolation and insight, of which the book offers plenty, but for which I had no personal resources to provide.

It is hard to describe the challenge this presented to me. I felt utterly helpless. Around that time, I found the memoir of a priest, Pierre Raphael, a follower of the desert saint Charles de Foucauld. Raphael served for many years as chaplain of Rikers Island, the famous prison in the East River between Manhattan and Brooklyn. "Why did I come to the prison and why did I stay here?" he wrote. "Because it is here that I need God the most."[3]

The difficulty of gaining entry to the jail, the challenges of the environment, and the encounters with the women suffering in it, all required resources beyond anything I had. That was the magnetic attraction of the thing. It was, in part, a burning desire to see the hidden parts of my culture and of myself. I wanted to see what lay in the dark and chaotic urban spaces hidden behind highways, as well as what lay in my own heart, behind the veil of my own middle-class self-satisfaction. That was a desire for reality, for truth, and to be changed in myself in accordance with that truth. Underneath that desire was a desire for a communion in human recognition, to recognize my humanity in the incarcerated women – and a hope that they might see theirs in mine.

I once met up with a college classmate who had spent his career providing legal defenses for those sentenced to death in a state where the death penalty is regularly imposed. I asked him about his work, and his face came alive. "We always lose. The prosecution has such better resources than we do," he said. "But my relationships with the convicted mean everything to me. I love my job." It was this sort of human connection in the midst of hopelessness that attracted and held me to jail ministry.

Such thinking is offensive to the mindset of rich and powerful do-gooders. We must – we *must* endeavor to make a difference, to win, to change the world, to get things right. What is difficult to see is that such thinking, even if it originates in real compassion, is ultimately patronizing or even tyrannical. It begins from a hidden fantasy of divine power, that the poor and their poverty depend on me, that benefit to others flows out from me, while I remain impassive and impermeable, receiving nothing. Mere words might be fruitless to break the spell of our imagined superiority. But it dissolves like wax before the fire in real life with poor people.

Every time I visited the jail, I chipped away at my inbuilt delusions of self-sufficiency. The suffering of the women was so great; what I had was so inadequate. I was no better than the people I served. What I had to offer them was what they would have to offer me, were the circumstances reversed. Their suffering could be mine; my comfort could be theirs. We all depended on God. They knew their dependence better than I did mine, since like most privileged people, I am prone to think of my resources as the reward due to my personal merits. As my illusions of superiority were worn down, often it seemed that I was the primary beneficiary of my volunteer work, as much or more than the women I served.

After two years, my jail ministry fell apart, thanks to the hostility of the jail officers and a new chaplain who hadn't yet learned the ropes. Shortly afterward, I began to discern religious life intensely. I struggled. I had gotten to know the Madonna House community through their house in Washington, DC. Their events were relaxed and homey; there was nothing to prove, and no one to impress. The conversations were serious, open, and profound. I never considered joining them, in part because I felt a need to use my intellectual training and talent, for which they had no outlet. (It was for this reason that I left the community years later.) But it is also true that I was repelled by their simplicity. Without titles or elaborate habits, without grand spaces in which to worship and artistic liturgies, they seemed simply to be middle-aged people active in their local parish. They had no prestige or status I could recognize.

At the same time, I studied theology with the Dominican friars, who had everything Madonna House did not: a beautiful Gothic chapel, flowing white habits, and prestige among the Catholics of the American Northeast. They were intellectually alive, reading, arguing, debating. Their intellectual life was not the point of their existence; it took place in between the height of priestly life, saying the liturgy, and the depths of humble service, counsel, advice, hearing confessions. I joked that I would impersonate a man to join them, following in the distinguished tradition of St. Pelagia and St. Marina.[4] Instead, they tried to help me to find a community of kindred women.

I visited five communities that I'd been told might welcome a woman intellectual. I found little appealing in any of them, except one. It was a new community for women modeled after the Dominican friars. On paper, it sang; in person, my instincts rebelled. After I crossed the last community off my list, I went to see my spiritual director. He forbade me to enter a community against my instincts – he told me it would make me miserable. I left his office in a rage and went across the street to hear Mass.

Mass was upstairs at the Basilica of the Immaculate Conception, a church with enormously high tiled ceilings and huge columns of beige marble. Vast, infinitely ornate mosaics covered the ceiling, angels and saints, stars, seas and whales. No matter what pew you choose, you are always lost in the crowd below and the air above. I knelt at whatever pew I was in. I burned with fury at anyone I could think of that might be blamed for my situation. I was particularly angry that the communities held out to me as for women intellectuals were nothing of the kind. As I saw it, Catholics had confused a woman intellectual with a woman who was also a high-powered professional. But it was just my high-powered professionalism that I was trying to flee.

I raged about the last community I had visited. "I've had better intellectual conversations at Madonna House!" I thought. Something in me stopped short. At that moment, the deacon was reading the Gospel, which turned out to be the section of the Sermon on the Mount called the Beatitudes:

> Blessed are the poor in spirit, for theirs is the kingdom of
>   heaven.
> Blessed are they who mourn, for they will be comforted.
> Blessed are the meek, for they shall inherit the earth.
> Blessed are they who hunger and thirst for righteousness,
>   for they will be satisfied.
> Blessed are the merciful, for they will be shown mercy.
> Blessed are the pure of heart, for they will see God.
> Blessed are the peacemakers, for they will be called
>   children of God.
> Blessed are they who are persecuted for righteousness'
>   sake, for theirs is the kingdom of heaven.[5]

I burst into tears. It was a song of total renunciation and, more than that, a pledge of divine love for the poor and the weak. The Beatitudes echo the Psalms: "The Lord hears the cry of the poor."[6] Somehow in my time serving the poor, I had developed a desire to be poor myself. But that desire for poverty went past material terms; it was a desire for a certain kind of helplessness. That is, I wanted to live in a way that recognized that I was, in truth, helpless. I wanted to see reality crash against my egotistical attempts to control and to manage everything. I had been trying to manage the character of my life, to tack on loving service to an intellectual center. But loving service had to be at the center, not the other way around. I had to go to Madonna House. It was the only place where I could lose everything that I cared about: where I would sacrifice not only the prospect of marriage or children, but all the trappings of the use of my mind, my education, and my zeal for learning. It terrified me just as the call to Abraham to sacrifice his son once had. But I had to follow the road as far as it would go. Otherwise, I would never be able to truly receive the kind of happiness promised in the Beatitudes. The love of God, according to the biblical authors, is freely offered to those who suffer; but the door is closed to those who stop their ears to the suffering of others.

————

I did not know it at the time, but like the story of the rich young man, the Beatitudes are a traditional call to the religious life. Symeon was a shepherd in a small village in Syria at the beginning of the fifth century CE. He went to a church with his family and, in the account of his contemporary, Theodoret,

> He told how he heard the Gospel utterance which declares blessed those who weep and mourn, wretched those who laugh, terms enviable those who possess a pure soul, and all the other blessings conjoined with them. He then asked one of those present what one should do to obtain each of these. He suggested the solitary life, and pointed to that consummate philosophy.[7]

Symeon studied this life with others, before devoting himself to a solitude and penance that even fellow ascetics found shocking. His reputation for holiness spread. Crowds came to him seeking a blessing from touching his garments. To avoid them, he had a pillar built on which to live – first six cubits high, then twelve, then twenty-two, and finally thirty-six. He lived on a pillar for a total of forty-eight years.[8]

The Beatitudes describe the poor, the humble and meek, the grief-stricken, and those who hunger and thirst for righteousness (because they do not have it) as "blessed." In English, "blessed" has a stench of false piety; it is often used as a sleight of hand to evade the unsettling paradox we have been trying to face. If we call someone "blessed," we do not need to ask if they are happy or successful. But without asking that question, we are hiding from something either unpleasant or uncomfortably strange.

In Greek, "blessed" is *makarios*: happy in the sense of lucky, fortunate, successful. It translates the "blessed" of the Psalms:

> Happy the man who has not sat in the council of the
>   ungodly...
> He is like a tree standing by the water, bearing fruit in
>   season.[9]

In the Hebrew Bible, too, the terms of happiness reverse conventional terms. The Psalms, like Jeremiah, Job, and Ecclesiastes, take place against the background of the commonplace order of things. In that commonplace order, the wicked are blessed. The unjust, the despoilers of widows and orphans, the greedy and arrogant, have lands and honors, children and livestock, power and reputation. Contrary to this appearance, the authors of the biblical texts write, it is the good man who flourishes. It is the just man – not the wicked man – who grows roots, who bears fruit. The wicked man, by contrast, will be blown away like chaff:

> I have seen the wicked triumphant,
> towering like a cedar of Lebanon.
> I passed by again; he was gone.
> I searched; he was nowhere to be found.[10]

One might read such passages as offering a promise to the righteous in real time: You will win out in the end, however it looks now; the tyrant flourishes now, but he will fall in the pit he digs himself. Or, as is sometimes suggested, God is his own reward. Justice is worth it, no matter what it costs you: "As for me, to be near God is my good, to make the LORD God my refuge."[11] By contrast, in the Beatitudes, Jesus seems to bite the bullet. It is not the just who are happy but the actually unhappy who are happy. It is those who suffer who receive – or is it that they notice? – God's goodness to them.

The Love of a Poor Man

Those who discern religious life, as I have suggested, are in love with God, in love with the poverty itself, in love with the Poor Man, Christ. But this is only part of the picture. In Christian teaching, the God they love also loves them – indeed, his love comes first, creating them in the womb and guiding their lives in providence.[12] How is his love recognized, and what role does it play in the call to religious life?

Kierkegaard tells a story of a wealthy king who falls in love with a peasant girl. He cannot raise her up to his place; if she were simply raised to his level as is, she would never feel at home. She may love her new royal status, thinking that she has hidden her shame from him. She would never know that he loves her for who she is in lowliness. Nor can he simply put on the clothes of the peasant; the earlier problem will reappear once his true identity is discovered. To persuade the peasant girl of his love, he must actually become a peasant himself, and the lowliest of peasants, the servant. Kierkegaard writes:

> But the form of the servant was not something put on. Therefore the god must suffer all things, endure all things, be tried in all things, hunger in the desert, thirst in his agonies, be forsaken in death, absolutely the equal of the lowliest of human beings – look, behold the man! The suffering of death is not his suffering, but his whole life is a story of suffering, and it is love that suffers, love that gives all and is itself destitute.[13]

The king mortifies his royalty to prove his own love, and hers. Instead of receiving royal love like prize for her merits, the peasant girl must accept that she is loved in lowliness alone. To truly love and receive love, we have to live the truth of who we are. Wealth does not really belong to us, and worse, it hides us from our true nature, giving us delusions of self-sufficiency, beneficence, and divinity. We see in the light of Christ and his love for us that we are not gods at all, but naked, helpless humans, totally dependent on grace.

It is easy for the philosophically inclined to be bewildered by the seeming indifference between subject and object that makes regular appearance in spiritual literature. Christ loves the poor; we are poor; he becomes poor; in love with him, we become poor like him. I have suggested so far that love of poverty is in part a desire for the truth about oneself, and in part a desire for the transcendent God who united himself with the poor.

———

The love of the Poor Christ for the lowliest human beings is testified by those among the poor who devote their lives to him. Like our wealthy subjects, the poor seek eternity and transcendence. But while their wealthy counterparts have their true humanity revealed to them, in all its weakness and vulnerability, for the poor, such vulnerability is beyond obvious. Without a need to be stripped of false pretenses, the poor receive the truth of their dignity and the loving care so often denied them by human beings.

The recognition of the suffering Christ as a fellow traveler with those who suffer is illustrated by an incident in the life of Kim Phuc Phan Thi. Kim was the child of a proud South Vietnamese family, who lived an idyllic childhood until her town was bombed with napalm by the South Vietnamese, targeting the Viet Cong who had forcibly infiltrated her village. The adults saw their shelter marked for bombing and sent the children out first to escape. Kim and the others ran into a cloud of napalm. Her uncle, a photographer for Associated Press, photographed her, her clothes burned off of her, running in agony. Her burns were so severe that she was left for dead in a morgue for two days.

After multiple operations, Kim returned to basic functioning, permanently marked by terrible scars and chronic pain. Thanks to the fame of her photograph, she was carefully minded and regularly put on display by the government after the war for propaganda purposes. As a university student, she became exhausted, isolated, and depressed to the point of suicide. One day she took refuge from the government minders in a library and looked through the religion section. She picked up and read through the Gospels and was struck by the suffering of Christ as the sign of his divinity. What was the purpose of his pain if he is not God? She recognizes him as "the wounded one, the one with scars." She leaves the faith of her family, becomes a Christian, and is disowned by her parents.[14]

The woman who came to be known as Josephine Bakhita was born to a loving family in Darfur, Sudan, in 1869. At the age of seven, she was kidnapped by slave traders. The traders called her "Bakhita," which in Arabic meant "Lucky." The cruel nickname replaced her original name, which along with her native language, was left in oblivion by the trauma of her violent kidnapping. After several years of imprisonment, scanty food, beatings, and torture, she was purchased by an Italian family. Her owners were kindly – at last, her life was free of violence – but they were blind to the horror of slavery. They traded her to another, less kindly Italian family in an exchange of favors.[15]

In the twenty years she was enslaved, Bakhita was polite and obedient to her masters. She obeyed them, in her own words, "as I did with my mother."[16] Only three times did she express her will contrary to her keepers. The first was when, while still a child imprisoned by traffickers, she escaped along with another child, only to be kidnapped and sold again. The second was when she insisted that her first Italian masters take her with them to Italy. Something about the name of the place enchanted her. They complied.

Her third choice was decisive: she was to be a free woman, and a nun. Her second Italian family left her in Italy with their child, while they returned to Sudan for business.

Bakhita and her ward were sent to a convent so that the child could learn her catechism. Bakhita was included in the classes, thanks to the intervention of a friend of the family. The friend gave her a silver crucifix. In Bakhita's words,

> As he gave me the crucifix he kissed it with devotion, then explained that Jesus Christ, the Son of God, had died for me. I did not know what the crucifix was, but I was moved by a mysterious power to keep it hidden, out of fear that the lady would take it away. I had never hidden anything before, because I had never been attached to anything. I remember that I looked at it in secret and felt something that I could not explain.[17]

When the family returned to take the two back to Sudan, Bakhita refused to go. She had drunk up the words of the catechists like water in the desert. She insisted that she continue her preparations for baptism. The family protested; even the sisters in the convent tried to change her mind. In Bakhita's words: "No, I will not leave the house of the Lord. It would mean my ruin."[18] The case went to the church authorities. The local magistrate, reviewing her case, noted that slavery was illegal in Italy. Bakhita was free.

Her local patron, who had given her the crucifix and encouraged her to become catechized, offered to adopt her as one of his children. She refused. There was one thing she wanted: to become a sister, to dedicate her life to prayer. So she did. For her, the convent was freedom – despite her alienation as the one non-white nun, and despite regular diminishment on account of her difference. "They want to see the beautiful beast," she mused of those who came to see her when she traveled on mission. During the time of these travels, she was often found in private, weeping and sighing. Explaining herself, she said: "They say 'poor little thing, poor little thing' But I am not a poor little thing, because I belong to the *Parón* [Venetian dialect for master] and I am in his house. Anyone who is not with the Lord, these are the poor ones."[19] For Bakhita, faith has transformed the meaning of authority – the freed slave calls God her "master" – and the meaning of poverty. To be poor, from her point of view, is to be without God.

The reports of Bakhita from those who knew her describe a woman with a profound contemplative core, who seemed always to be attending to God in her heart, as she went about her tasks. She spent hours in adoration in the convent chapel. Once, left alone there for some hours, a sister asked her if she was tired after staying there so long. Bakhita replied, "Not at all! I have been having a wonderful time with Him. He has waited so long for me."[20]

Bakhita fled violent injustice for the religious life. So did Margaret of Castello, several hundred years earlier.[21] Margaret was born to a noble family in the year 1287, blind, dwarfed, with a hunch and a limp. Her parents, horrified, built a dungeon for her so that her existence would not shame them to their noble friends. Like Bakhita, Margaret had a single friend: the family chaplain, who catechized her. Eventually, even the dungeon was insufficient to placate her parents. They brought her to a shrine at Castello, in hopes that she would be healed of her infirmities. She was not healed. They abandoned her, blind and alone, in the church, and went back to their own lands.

Margaret lived at first among the poor of Castello, traveling from shelter to shelter. At last, a convent received her, one with lax rules, that did not observe silence, where the nuns received gifts and chitchatted regularly with outsiders. If shelter was what Margaret wanted, this more relaxed environment might have suited her well. But she wanted to encounter God in silence and self-denial. Her protests to that effect led to her expulsion from the convent. She found refuge at last as a Dominican tertiary, a member of a lay community attached to the local Dominican friars. Finding the last room she was offered too luxurious, she insisted on sleeping in the garret for the rest of her days.[22]

An enslaved person and a homeless woman with disabilities might seem to have obvious motives for religious life: for the first, there is freedom, and for the second, a caring home. Yet Bakhita was offered adoption, with a dowry, into a well-to-do Italian family, and she refused it. Margaret was thrown out of her first community for following the rule; if she had wanted only a home, it would have been rational for her to accommodate herself to their greater freedoms. These women, too, are in love with God, the eternal and transcendent, who for them is a source of dignity they are denied elsewhere. It is God, and God alone, who cares for them without condition. While a single friend, a single social worker, a single organization or program can provide care for a certain time and in a certain place, God provides one friend, one place, one event after another, in the circumstances ordained by providence, providing in one person or event or another exactly what is needed, leading those in need to love and contemplation of himself.

Poverty as Atonement for Wealth

I suggested that for me, volunteering in jail was a way to chastise the ruthless ambition with which I had climbed the social ladder, and to mortify my pretenses of divine self-sufficiency and control over my destiny and the destinies of others. By long tradition, religious life is a refuge for sinners, a path to atonement.

The protagonist of the film *The Island* (*Ostrov*) (2006) is a sailor in the Russian navy in the Second World War. He and an officer are stranded on an island on the Baltic, where a Nazi ship soon arrives. The sailor betrays his own presence and then, begging the Nazis for his life, betrays the location of his officer. The Nazis order him to shoot his own officer; he begs and pleads, unable to shoot. In the end, he fires, and the officer falls backward off the ship and into the sea. The sailor is left on shore. The Nazis detonate his ship; his wounded body is collected by monks and taken to a nearby monastery. He spends the rest of his life in prayer and penance, in atonement for his cowardice and for the death of the officer.

The great and ancient stories of the repentance of sex addicts and prostitutes show lives of atonement. St. Mary of Egypt seduced a boat full of pilgrims to Jerusalem, before having a face-to-face encounter with an icon of the Virgin that sent her into the desert for the rest of her days.[23] Pelagia of Antioch, so attractive that no man could see her without falling in love with her, passes by the bishop Nonnus and seven fellow bishops, in her full majesty. Seeing her, they look away; but Nonnus is deeply struck. He speaks to his fellow bishops of her, seeking their prayers.

Nonnus is particularly moved by how much time and trouble she has taken to beautify herself, and how little trouble, comparatively speaking, he has spent on the pursuit of goodness, virtue, and the things of God. The fervor with which he feels this insight fills his next Sunday homily. By chance, Pelagia herself has felt drawn to go to church that day. She is reduced to tears by Nonnus's homily and begs for baptism. She gives away all of the riches gained from her previous life, to be given to the orphans and widows, the poor and the destitute, so that "what was sin's wealth shall henceforth be righteousness' treasury." Departing the city, Pelagia dresses as a man and becomes a monk.[24]

The examples so far have been of sinners with particular crimes or vices on their conscience. But atonement is not simply self-inflicted punishment. Atonement can also be seen more simply, as a means of changing the heart. If freely chosen, atonement instills a disposition of character, contrary to the harmful one, for its own sake. The selfishness of greed may be counterbalanced by careful attention to the needs of the destitute. The sins of exploitative lust may be counterbalanced by modesty and true charity and self-sacrifice. It is reparation and transformation through love, a form of healing. Atonement means to repair our faults more than to inflict the pain they deserve. Those who atone seek to be healed by rejecting a false front or a double life. They offer themselves as a humble and weak human being in service to others because this is what, in Christian teaching, a human being is. Lives of atonement, then, are much like other Christian lives. Since all are sinners, all guilty of the original sin – pretense to divinity – no special stain or mark is attached.

Atonement can be undertaken not only for one's own sins but for the sins of others. When I went to jail, I sought to overcome my worst qualities and open myself up to something different and better. But I also sought to atone in some small way for the cruelty and neglect with which the women there were treated by others. A theme in the prayers of the eastern Christian churches is that I, the one praying, have sinned in all the ways anyone else has sinned. Before communion in the liturgy of St, John Chrysostom, one addresses Christ: "You are truly the Christ, the Son of the living God, who came into the world to save sinners, of whom I am the greatest." Orthodox author Olivier Clement writes that there is nothing hyperbolic or rhetorical about this claim to be the greatest of sinners. Rather it reflects the grace of perceiving "the ontological unity of the human race." I am not a merely good or bad individual but share my substance with every human being.[25]

Strictly speaking, the unity of mankind is something mystical, and atonement is in its essence a mystical process. The whole of humanity, for Christians, is one body, the body of Christ. Thanks to that hidden unity, any human being can atone for the sins of any other, following on Christ's atonement for the sins of all. From the suffering of a single person, if the suffering servant consents to his or her circumstances, divine assistance or grace is released for others. Sin is a debt that can be repaid, not with money but with conversion of heart, silence, suffering, and service. The world has a hidden order where suffering and injustice are actually repaired by such acts, through the grace they release through secret channels.

For all the mysticism at its core, I think that the unity of the human race is perceptible at the human level. What is the shock that Martin of Tours feels when, cozy in his winter cloak, he sees someone shivering with cold? What mars the happy-go-lucky wealth of Francis of Assisi if not the fact that so many suffer in poverty? Further from an explicitly Christian context, James Baldwin describes Shakespeare's love of humanity as:

> knowing, which is not the same as understanding, that whatever was happening to anyone was happening to him.[26]

A public atonement can be an act of communication, a way of undoing a public crime. Consider a fantasy atonement I have long dreamt of for the financiers who crush dreams through fraud and recklessness, who eat the wealth of families and laugh all the way to the bank. In real life, such criminals are permitted to live and work without consequence or penalty, even after their misdeeds are exposed to the public. Their pretense at superiority to their victims endures in public, is even reinforced, as if it were something real and true. But suppose they were struck with remorse, or suppose our culture was healthy enough to have a leader, a prophet or priest, who could sentence a wrongdoer to atonement. They might be sent to serve personally those who suffer most: cleaning bathrooms for the incarcerated, washing the feet of the homeless, changing bedpans for the bedridden. Would it not be fitting for them to do so? It might communicate as public punishment does, that the dignity of the victims cannot be denied without challenge.

The wrongdoer's pretense to a higher-than-ordinary form of humanity is humbled and shattered by the punishment. Such a public spectacle also aids all of us complicit in their actions, whether by cooperation, encouragement, or indifference. We are invited to see ourselves in them. Nor would atonement be a mere spectacle; it can be reasonably expected to have a concrete effect, to change hearts or shift habits and modes of character.

I have treated poverty as something desirable in itself for the wealthy who choose religion, and as something transformed in its nature by those who come to religion from poverty. But in Christian tradition wealth and comfort are seen as inherently dangerous, as our earlier passage from Revelation about lukewarmness suggested. In Luke's version of the Beatitudes, the blessing pronounced on the poor is followed by curses on the rich.[27] Some wealthy Christians turn to religious life to atone for the sins and crimes associated with wealth. As I explained earlier, I was myself drawn to serve the poor, in part, because of a sense that my relative wealth had obscured my vision of myself and had built walls between myself and the reality of the sufferings of others, sufferings in which in some sense I was complicit.

George Eliot's *Middlemarch*, following a great theme of nineteenth-century novels, studies the corrupting power of wealth on individuals. The young and decent Fred Vincy is in love with a clever and wonderful woman, but he haphazardly sacrifices his chances through his love of fine horses and good times, his smug assumption of a large inheritance, and through the strategic inability to calculate his own debts. The doctor Lydgate, determined in integrity and devotion to medicine for the sake of humanity, falls into debt thanks to his wife. In the resulting anxiety, he lets his integrity slip when a life is at stake. Wealth threatens even the central and sympathetic characters of the novel, those for whom we hold out hope of their happiness or at least their goodness. Even the saintly Farebrother has a weakness for gambling, exacerbated by his poverty. By contrast, the wealthy Bulstrode, something close to a villain, has lied, betrayed, and left the righteous destitute, all for his longing to be powerful and respectable.

We also know that wealth moves with laws of its own, independent of the virtues, vices, or intentions of individuals. It is not farfetched to see "the world" – the locus of competition for power and status – as the world made by our struggle over our material conditions. As such, it is perhaps the greatest engine of evil we know. In the great age of wealth, when exploration, global trade, and the growth of industry took shape, the greatest dehumanizations have taken place: the sending of the English poor to Australia, the brutal repression of the Irish, the Belgian conquest of the Congo, the grisly, centuries-long African slave trade.

The extraordinary wealth of North America and Europe creates an illusion of global prosperity, similar to the everyday illusion that our works will endure forever. In most American cities, the poor are carefully hidden from view; transit lines come to a halt outside wealthy neighborhoods to keep the rabble and the sight of them out. Thanks to globalization, the poverty relied on to produce our inexpensive goods is now also hidden in other countries, and in

the remoter corners of those countries, in the trash heaps
and refugee camps and shantytowns of the world.

Our modern-day famines are less a matter of
drought and soil failure as catastrophes that follow in the
wake of war, as in Yemen and Afghanistan. War itself is
fought for profit, as suggested by the famous concern of
Dwight D. Eisenhower,[28] in the tradition of the ancient
corruption of the warlord Agamemnon. We hear so much
about the evils of colonialism gone by that it can escape
notice how our current lifestyles also rely on the cheap and
dangerous labor of the desperate and destitute. It is widely
known that the lithium-ion batteries in laptops, smart-
phones, and electric cars are made with cobalt, mined by
children and other vulnerable people in the Democratic
Republic of the Congo, at risk of death and permanent
injury.[29] Our multinational technology companies have
turned the world's refugee camps into the extremely cheap
labor needed to label data for their algorithms.[30]

To catch a glimpse of the horrors in which all of us
are complicit, on which all of our material flourishing
depends, is to be struck with both helplessness and hopelessness. Emerging from ignorant bliss, it is natural enough to
be enraged. Yet anger, however worthy, must be used well.
We can generate imaginary dramas in which our righteousness is the star. We may put on a performance for our own
benefit or the benefit of our in-group. Anger, if taken up
from a position of power or superiority, degenerates into
bad faith. Our emotions substitute for actions. Our focus
turns away from ourselves and our surroundings – say, those
who suffer in our own communities – and onto imaginary

scenes where, not coincidentally, we are unable to effect any change. Anger alone does not touch the suffering for which we are responsible, nor does it necessarily free us from delusions of grandeur.

One sign of an authentic anger, an anger in good faith, is the recognition that the victim of poverty, of war or injustice is separated from me by the slightest of chances. One way to cultivate that recognition, as I have suggested, is to live with the poor. Another is, like the religious, to become poor oneself.

The righteous anger of Catherine de Hueck Doherty, foundress of Madonna House, and the role it played in her deliberate, self-aware atonement for the sins of the rich, will be helpful here. She was aided in her insights, I think, by the violent contingencies of the early twentieth century, which tossed her and her family up and down social classes like a ship in a storm. Catherine was born into a well-to-do family in pre-revolutionary Russia in 1896 and married into nobility at the age of fifteen.[31] She was known ever thereafter as "the Baroness". After the 1917 Revolution, Catherine and her husband fled to their Finland estate. The local people welcomed them with pitchforks, so to speak, and undertook to starve them to death. They were trapped without regular food for three months: a few frozen potatoes, a few fish from the lake. They gnawed on firewood. Catherine's teeth loosened and her hair fell out. She prayed to God: "If you save me from this, in some way I will offer my life to you." She fell unconscious and awoke, having been rescued by anti-Communist forces.[32] They traveled destitute, as refugees, first to the UK and then to Canada, where they had a son.

In Canada, Catherine's husband preoccupied himself with what he could find of good living, gambling, and women. Catherine took any job she could find, working as a laundress, a cleaning lady, waiting tables. She moved to New York City for more opportunities and took up similar work there, sending what money she earned back to her family. Eventually, she got a break. She found work on the Chatauqua, the traveling variety show in the 1920s, hamming it up as a dethroned aristocrat who knew the horrors of Communism face to face. From there, she took up a good job with a lecture bureau.[33]

Living in Toronto, middle class again, with her son, Catherine was disquieted. She had caught a glimpse of something in her years of poverty that she did not want to lose sight of. She wanted to be poor again: to give away her wealth and to live in a small apartment in a poor neighborhood, fasting and praying. Eventually she received permission from her bishop to do so. She began to work with the working people of Toronto and to respond to their needs during the Depression, setting up a library, a soup kitchen, and reading groups on the papal encyclicals that proclaimed the dignity of labor. Young people joined her; she called the community "Friendship House."

Catherine moved to Harlem in New York City in 1938 to found a new Friendship House based on interracial justice. She lived in a poor apartment with bare necessities. She got to know the local people, their strengths, and their needs. She used the social status granted arbitrarily by her skin color to bully and upbraid local Catholic officials to integrate their schools, universities, and parishes.

Catherine regularly longed for anonymity; it was one of the faces of her beloved poverty. She escaped her community to travel to an unknown town and work as a waitress. She returned to marry for a second time. Shortly after, they moved to Combermere, Ontario, to serve the rural poor. She worked as a nurse, helping mothers in desperate poverty to give birth. Young people came to her, and so a new community was formed; in 1947 Madonna House was founded; as time went on, they developed commitments to poverty and obedience, as well as to celibacy. As Catherine grew older, she sought more and more the contemplative heart of poverty and service, and wrote both of the littleness of a human act of will and the vast landscape of divine love it opened up.[34]

It was no coincidence that it was Madonna House that attracted me to religious life. When I first read about Catherine Doherty, she struck me as someone familiar. She was a bit older than my grandparents and had shared some of their suffering and their experiences. She was a reader, well-traveled, urbane, and sophisticated, as my grandparents had been. Like them, she had witnessed wars of astonishing violence that shattered nations and empires, that consigned to oblivion whole cultures and ways of life. Yet unlike anyone in my family, she had a deep faith in Christianity from her childhood and interpreted all of these events in its light.

I have suggested that the choice of poverty reveals who we truly are. It is a way to depend on God, to give up one's attempts at control, and to test one's motivations. If I am in love with a rich man, but before I commit myself to him, he loses his wealth, my love will be revealed for what it is. In this way, poverty clarifies and purifies one's own motivations. Likewise, the choice of poverty promises a sort of communion with the poor and the suffering, as well as an identification with and imitation of the Christ who made himself poor.

Under the aspect of faith, even a small act of will matters, a withdrawal of consent to the machinery of evil. This may appear to be a self-seeking vanity, a pretense of purity. It may be so for a given individual, but it need not be so, and it need not remain so. The cultivation of one's own character, to burn out greed and to cultivate compassion and humility, if practiced writ large, would transform the surrounding community. Even if the "writ large" is not under our control, it is worthwhile to play one's part. To live off of the land, like Benedictines or Cistercians, or to live by donations, like the Franciscans or Dominicans, is to renounce the world of moneymaking, to build an alternate world, however slow and inefficacious it may appear. Call it "the kingdom of God."

3   Intimacy with God

> Prayer is the conjoining of man and God in unity. It means actual reconciliation with God, the mother of tears and also their daughter, the forgiveness of sins, the bridge to pass over tribulations and a support to our weakness. It puts away devilish wars, it is the work of angels, the food for those who need charity, happiness, the work that is beneficial, the core of virtues, and the giver of other gifts. It is nourishment for our souls, light to our minds, filling for our days, proof of our hope, our grace, the treasure of monks, and the repository of the silent in serenity. (Pope Kyrillos VI)[1]

The deliberate choice of poverty is a sacrifice, an action against one's instincts in order to seek a higher good. We are all acquainted with garden-variety asceticism: We renounce eating certain foods for the sake of health or good looks; we willingly undergo the pain of exercise for fitness or for the thrill of athletic excellence; we give up sleep for years on end to nurture a child. The central difficulty in grasping Christian asceticism, at least for non-believers, is the transcendence of its goal and the ultimate mysticism bound into the workings of sacrifice. I find it simplest, and truest, to explain Christian asceticism as the discipline of true love. As Paul writes:

> If I give away everything I own, and if I hand over my
> body to be burned, and have not love, I gain nothing.[2]

We are familiar with sacrifices for concrete loved ones: sleep for children, as I say, but also wealth or ambition for the sake of a spouse's happiness; the sacrifice of a preference for the common peace; the sacrifice of peace and quiet so that others may pursue their activities; the sacrifice of time, trouble, pride, and comfort that all of us know well, if we have ever tried to love anyone. Those who love are plagued by worry; they sacrifice their peace of mind. Anxiety for the beloved can consume a person for the lifetime of their connection, and past it. Such worry is a natural outcome of any unconditional love. The one who chooses to love chooses to accept the shared pain of any harm to their beloved, and ultimately, their loss in death. Love requires the projected acceptance of debilitating grief.

By contrast with the natural human goal to love those who belong to one's family, neighborhood, village, town, or nation, the Christian goal is to love God and one's neighbor as oneself. Such love, called "charity" in English, is a virtue, a studied condition of the heart and mind, not a feeling. As the love of God, it involves exercising one's will against feelings of anger, hostility, mistrust, pride, fear, self-satisfaction, and boredom. As the love of one's neighbor, charity involves acting in spite of feelings of dislike, disdain, repugnance, anger, bitterness, and all the other feelings that divide us each from the other. Christian love is a concrete source of action, a living commitment to devote oneself to God and to do good to each and every human being one encounters.

In the ordinary course of life, a given love for a given beloved precedes the discipline of love. We fall in love, or the baby is born, or, as small children, our parents come into view. Once touched, we become capable of sacrifice. But to love God is to love someone omnipresent since one's birth, and whose will is expressed in all the people and circumstances of life. To love one's neighbor means to love whomever happens to be in front of you. One might choose such a love thanks to a striking experience, just as in romantic love, like Francis with the leper. But it is possible for us, shaped by whatever love we have received in life, to set aside loves competing with God and neighbor in an act of total renunciation. Such love is unlimited in principle, and so is the renunciation it requires.

Christian asceticism, like all asceticism, is the careful cultivation of the objects of our attention. Left to ourselves, our eyes are filled with memes, ads, pornography, candy wrappers, signs of wealth and status. By default, our ears filled with noise, the push and prod of invitation, entreaty, advertising, insults, demands, flattery, contempt, guilt-trips. Our hearts may immerse themselves in food, entertainment, or narcotics, reducing other human beings to simple instruments to our petty satisfactions. Our default self-absorption is only occasionally interrupted by sudden predilections for the good of others, unless we choose to restrain it and to cultivate other human elements in its stead.

All love requires sacrifice; but charity requires total renunciation. I have begun with the sacrifice of wealth, with chosen poverty, but religious life demands many more renunciations: the sacrifice of sex, children, and the pleasures of

intimacy, along with sacrifice of the exercise of one's preferences in companions, daily routine, diet, entertainment, place
of residence, and line of work. What is the point? What lies at
the other end of the sacrifice? Where is the disciplined attention directed? How is the love of God and neighbor lived out
in a real life? I begin from the most attractive ascetic practices,
found at the core of the religious life: silence and solitude.

Silence

When I walked into Sunday Mass in Auburn, Alabama, in
the spring of 2005, I knew immediately that I wanted to be
Catholic. The church was sunlit, with long shadows, and two
golden angels leaned over the tabernacle against a sky-blue
wall. I found myself in the midst of a gathering of human
beings that appeared completely random: families, solitaries,
groups of friends; of every skin color, from every part of the
world, from various social classes and walks of life. The
variety suggested an unusual common purpose beyond
ordinary gatherings for human enterprise, entertainment,
or comfort. Over that common purpose was silence, the
silence of the parishioners kneeling in their pews, preparing
for Mass.

  The silence of a church, like the silence of nature, is
compatible with some noise, sound, or quiet chitchat. It is
not absence of sound, but a sound all its own. By contrast,
the silence of nature is absent of human noise. Instead of the
buzz of machinery, instead of traffic, shouting, the sounds of
large-scale human movement, we hear the wind in the trees,
the lapping of water on the shore, birdsong. The silence of a

church or the silence of a monastery is not the sound of absence, but the sound of restraint. It is the sound of the choice not to speak.

Silence is not emptiness. If it were, we would seek it in solitude in outer space or on such terrestrial landscapes that most resemble it: the arctic tundra for instance. Human silence draws us in more readily. What is attractive, what is resonant or consoling, about the human choice not to speak?

Not all human silences are attractive, resonant, or consoling. Consider the silence met by a suffering inmate in a prison or the awful silence that follows a letter from an abuse victim who has decided at long last to speak. The chosen silence when a word is needed is among the worst human failures, not a human achievement. Walter Ciszek describes the "constantly terrifying" "tomb-like" quiet of the KGB prison, Lubianka, where the guards wore special cloth shoes so as not to be heard approaching one's cell.[3]

The restraint of silence mysteriously resembles other key forms of religious restraint. The poet Charles Peguy wrote a series of poems written from God's perspective. In the poem called "*Liberté*" (Freedom), God tenderly admires the strong person knelt in prayer.

> When you have once known what it is to be loved freely, submission no longer has any taste.
> All the prostrations in the world
> Are not worth the beautiful upright attitude of a free man as he kneels.[4]

Kneeling is also a form of restraint. One is not standing, set out in motion, ready to attack or to retreat. One is not sitting, taking one's place as a member of a meeting or council. The stance is deliberate helplessness, chosen submission. Freedom and strength are built into self-denial, renunciation, and sacrifice.

I suspect that the restraint of silence, of kneeling, of the deliberate choice against action, assertion, aggrandizement, and aggression, is essential to the beauty of the religious life. Consider the stories of religious sacrifice so beloved by the faithful. The actress Dolores Hart, star of the silver screen, paired with Elvis Presley, chooses to sacrifice all for life as a Benedictine nun.[5] Augustine sacrifices his blossoming career as a Roman civil servant for a quiet life of philosophy – and as it turns out, tedious episcopal service to a North African diocese.[6] Antony and Doña Casilda shine in the light of their sacrificed wealth and comfort. The sacrifice of a life, like silence, bears the ghost of the thing it restrains; the countervailing expectations trail it like a shadow, beautiful through contrast.

What is the object of this silence or this sacrifice? On a visit to the US Naval Academy, across the street from my chaotic little liberal arts college, I watched some hundreds of midshipmen file into the dining hall for lunch in neat rows, without saying a word. If an army in formation inspires awe, it is surely for its restraint. Young men and women who might be shouting in drunken revelry are uniformed, straight, and silent, by their own choice.

The awe inspired by a silent row of nuns or monks filing into choir seems to be something similar to military silence. It is awe at restraint as such: the restraint of the ballet dancer, the choice *not* to act, do, or say. Such restraint is powerful. A group of monks led by St. Odo were traveling over the Alps in the late tenth century. Robbers lay in wait for them, but the gang leader was astounded at the sight of men in habits, with downcast eyes, reciting the psalms. "I never remember seeing men like these before," he muttered. The robbers left the monks undisturbed.[7]

The difference between the splendor of military silence and the splendor of religious silence is one of *ends*. For what purpose does one restrain oneself? For military communities, it is martial discipline, aimed at the virtues of war and the practicalities of effectiveness on the battlefield. Silence aims at focus, at narrowing one's perceptions to a greater acuity where matters of life, danger, rescue or ruin are concerned. I have never had a major surgery, but I would expect and hope that surgeons practice a similar silence. Were I wheeled into a raucous operating room, with loud laughter, refreshments, and festive music, I would fear for my life.

Here we run into the central feature, so puzzling and so splendid, of religious restraint. It is directed primarily at an invisible being, God. The men and women, kneeling at prayer, seek God's help, God's insight, God's victory on the battlefield. Who or what is God?

God Speaks

The silence of monasteries is not total, but selective. Instead of the typical noise of demands for attention, chitchat, gossip, dumb jokes, posturing, arguments, advertising, the monk or the nun hears the words of the Bible and the prayers of the liturgy. An old tradition of Roman Catholic monasteries begins a Great Silence after the final prayer of the evening, broken only by the next hour of prayer. Speech during the day is for the purpose of necessary communication. Otherwise, the speaking is only the Word, the scriptures recited at the hours of prayer or read aloud by a single reader during meals.[8] In this way, the most obvious manifestation of God in a religious community is through God's words.

God speaks, according to Christian tradition, through the words of the Bible. That tradition is partly one of divine authorship, that these words were inspired by the Holy Spirit. But the scriptures are also the word of God because they are most centrally the words of Christ himself, the God made man. The Gospels and the words of Jesus from the Last Supper play a central role in Christian liturgy. The Psalms are also central, through the Liturgy of the Hours, where monks or nuns pray all 150 psalms in a weekly or monthly cycle, divided into prayers five times a day. The earliest Christian writers understood the Psalms as spoken through the mouth of Christ, following the example of his words from the cross, the opening of Psalm 22, "My God, my God, why have you abandoned me?"[9] In the Psalms, the whole range of human feeling and experience is condensed and put before God in the form of prayers. The prayers are frank and honest, complaining of injustice, suffering, enmity, and loneliness; they express fear, awe, wonder, contrition, and tenderness. The Bible, then, is meant to be a kind of sanctification of the whole range of human experience, the showing of it in relation to God and in light of God's goodness.

The words and phrases of the Bible have a remarkable history in their effects on the hearers. Antony heard the gospel of the rich young man as a direct, personal instruction. So Augustine, thinking of Antony, is drawn to pick up the letters of Paul after hearing a child's voice in a garden. He reads Romans 13:3:

> Not in rioting and drunkenness, not in chambering and impurities, not in contention and envy, but put ye on the Lord Jesus Christ and make no provision for the concupiscence of the flesh.

Augustine immediately commits himself to celibacy.[10] It is this moment, not Augustine's earlier intellectual persuasion that Christianity is true, that he considers his conversion. The pilgrim of the Russian spiritual classic *The Way of a Pilgrim* hears 1 Thessalonians read in church, the exhortation to "pray always," and spends the rest of his life praying always. I heard the Beatitudes in this way: not only as a personal address, but as one that named who and what I was, like the oracle at Delphi: This is what you are: poor, meek, dependent on God, and beloved, showered with good things.

The immediacy of the words of the scriptures in the ears of believers is what the author of the letter to the Hebrews seems to describe when he calls the word of God "living and effective." The words of God unveil ourselves to ourselves:

> For the word of God is living and active, more cutting than any two-edged sword, reaching even to the divide between soul and spirit, joints and marrow, and able to discern reflections and thoughts of the heart. No creature

> is concealed from him, but everything is naked and
> exposed to the eyes of him to whom we render an
> account.[11]

Here the words of God are not only a means of self-examination and self-exposure for our own sake, but help us to reveal ourselves in relationship to God, so that our communion is true, honest, and wholehearted, without artifice.

For someone's words to strike one to the core is certainly a sign of intimacy, friendship, or love. Still, the picture is incomplete: Transformative words may, after all, come from another human being, a dead poet, a teacher, or a taxi driver, with whom one has no enduring relationship. What makes it possible for the transformative words to be a part of a two-way relationship, as the Hebrews passage suggests? What sort of friendship or intimacy is possible between God and myself, given that God cannot be seen or touched, an entirely different kind of being than I am? To approach these questions, we turn from silence to solitude.

Solitude

Catherine of Siena, the twenty-third of twenty-five children, seemed to come into the world already possessed of an intense piety. At the age of six, she stopped in the middle of the street, overwhelmed by a vision. She saw, hanging in the air above the Dominican church, a regal bridal chamber in which Christ sat enthroned, surrounded by Peter, Paul, and John the Evangelist. Christ gazed at her and blessed her with the sign of the cross. The vision disappeared only when she was interrupted by her brother. A few years later, still a young girl, she was struck by a longing for solitude and, taking a loaf of bread, went out in search of it. She found the edge of a wilderness and took shelter for a time in a cave. She returned home, too young yet to undertake the training for her vocation.

Catherine insisted on staying unmarried, against her parents' wishes, cutting off her beautiful hair to prove she was serious. She lived for some years in a small cell in their home, fasting, praying, doing penance, leaving the house only to attend liturgies or to serve the sick. The cell, in Catherine's mind, was her bridal chamber.

One Lent, nearing the end of her time of solitude and at the beginning of her more public life, Christ himself appeared to her with his saints and betrothed her to himself with a ring that only she could see.[12] The physical cell, the little room with its four walls, was only an aid to the enclosure of her heart, which she reserved wholeheartedly for Christ as her lover and her spouse.

Solitude is the place of prayer, of conversation between a human being and God. It is also a place of intimacy. Ordinary marriage has as its central location the bedroom, the home, the little cottage where two live as one. To give oneself to someone else involves a withdrawal from everything else, a space of privacy. The cell or the hermitage, in the religious life, is just this meeting place, the enclosure that shuts out everything that is not the beloved. The inner room is free from distractions, objects of attention that conflict with true and unconditional love. When we meet our beloved in solitude, we communicate that they are not mere decoration or badge of honor, but worthy of the whole of our attention, the whole of our heart. The enclosure serves, then, a variety of purposes: as a school for whole-heartedness, a test of commitment, a place where authenticity is sought and proved, and finally, as a place of communion and intimate connection.

The call to solitude for prayer has long roots into the Hebrew Bible. Jacob, in the book of Genesis, must sleep in solitude as he travels from home for the first time, fleeing the wrath of his brother Esau and seeking a new life with his mother's relatives. Lying down to rest, he sees a ladder to God with angels ascending and descending. God stands beside him and promises him that his offspring will cover the earth.[13] Years later, returning from his uncle's home with his wives, children, and vast livestock, Jacob separates himself from his goods and his family, hoping to protect them from Esau, whom he is en route to meet. Once again spending the night in a desert solitude, Jacob wrestles with a mysterious stranger until dawn. Jacob prevails in the struggle, and before departing, the stranger tells him he has "wrestled with gods and men and prevailed." Jacob himself saw it as a place he had "seen God face to face."[14]

In the New Testament, Jesus is seen to pray in solitude from the beginning of his public life, which begins in forty days alone in the desert.[15] He regularly retreats from crowds as well as the small band of his disciples to a mountain to pray.[16] In the Sermon on the Mount, Jesus instructs his followers as to how to give alms, how to fast, and how to pray. All three kinds of devotion, he says, must be done privately, in secret:

> When you pray, do not be like the hypocrites, who love
> to pray while standing in the synagogues and on the
> street corners so that others may see them ... But when
> you pray, go to your inner room [*tamieion*], close the
> door, and pray to your Father in secret. And your Father
> who sees in secret will repay you.[17]

Jesus's words call for privacy in matters of God. In one
sense, the privacy is ascetical, meant to purify motives by
removing their objects and so to dull their satisfactions.
Does one pray for the approval of others? That motivation
can be mortified by praying in privacy.

In private the truth comes out. This is so even in
cases of extreme hypocrisy: When one's private life is a
double life, what is kept in secret reveals what is authentic
about us, the truth of what we care about. The nature of
privacy can be illustrated by a brief digression into the
meaning of the word "inner room," *tamieion* in Greek.[18]

The word *tamieion* in older, classical Greek means a
storeroom for household goods, a pantry, a barn, or a treasury
where wealth is kept;[19] or in metaphorical usage, a storehouse
in the soul for knowledge or virtue.[20] In the Septuagint, the
ancient translation of the Hebrew Bible into Greek, perhaps
the text closer than any to the authors of the New Testament,
the meaning becomes more general. The Hebrew word translated there, *cheder*, is simply any private or enclosed space.
When Joseph is regent of Egypt, and his brothers come
begging for grain, he hides his identity from them but is
overwhelmed by emotion. He sends out his attendants, goes
into a *tamieion*, and weeps.[21] Many years later, God sends a
plague of frogs on the Egyptians, so many frogs that they make

their way into the *tamieia to koitônôn*, the private sleeping rooms.[22] Elsewhere, a *tamieion* is a room where enemies might lie in ambush;[23] where one might lock oneself in to relieve oneself;[24] a room where a sick or elderly person lies;[25] a hiding place from enemies.[26]

What happens in the private room may not stay private; for instance, the anointing of Jehu as king.[27] More important: What a king says in his *tamieion*, his bedchamber, is heard by the prophet Elisha.[28] In Luke's version of the Sermon on the Mount, Jesus says that "what is whispered in one's *tamieion* will be proclaimed on the housetops" that is, "nothing concealed will not be revealed, nor secret that will not be known."[29]

The *tamieion* of the Septuagint is also a place for erotic intimacy. The lover of the *Song of Songs* will meet the king in his *tamieion* for a tryst, or will bring her lover to the *tamieion* of her mother, where the speaker was conceived.[30] When the protagonist of the book of Tobit is betrothed to Sarah, his beloved, her parents prepare a *tamieion* for her. Her mother weeps over her there, expecting Tobit to die as her previous betrotheds have. In the room together they pray in thanksgiving for their marriage. They spend the night together and are both found alive and asleep the next day, to the joy of the family.[31]

Lastly, the *tameion* as the space of intimacy and privacy is used in an extended sense for the inner parts of ourselves. In Proverbs, we find:

> The lamp of the LORD is our breath
> it searches the chambers [*tamieia*] within.[32]

In other words, just as our breath plumbs the depths of our bodies, the light of God – however we understand that – shows up what is in the depths of our hearts and minds, our hidden dreams, motivations, intentions, and plans. Augustine, mentioning the Sermon on the Mount in his commentary on the psalms, remarks, "The heart is the bedroom."[33]

The inner room is a space of intimacy, of bodily function, illness, and lovers' trysts, a place where we are vulnerable. It is where we hide our shame, our nakedness, our weakness, and our secret thoughts and intentions. Delilah hides a Philistine ambush in the house with Samson, but even more, she hides from him her true loyalties. The inner room is also a place of exposure: where the truth comes out. In the ancient Jewish text the Psalms of Solomon, "God knows the inner chambers [*tamieia*] of the heart before they come about," that is to say, our secret thoughts and intentions.[34] Our inner selves may be hidden from others, just like the inner folds of our lungs – but God sees them with his lamp, and they will one day be exposed from the rooftops, good or bad, beautiful or ugly. Such exposure, in the Bible, is judgement – it is what is revealed or exposed when one is tested.

I have suggested that solitude functions both as a school of wholeheartedness and as a space of union or communion, for intimacy with God. Just as in the analogy of human romantic love, revelation, nakedness, vulnerability, and honesty are deeply connected to communion and intimacy. One goes to meet God within the confines of one's own heart. The strangeness of the presence within myself of the eternal, transcendent God, as someone who can be sought when I am by myself, is puzzled over by Augustine in his great meditation on memory in the tenth book of *Confessions*. What strange link could there be between my own mind and heart and the God who is beyond everything? I will not be able to dispel the mystery here, but I will circle around it in an attempt to make some progress toward it. To do so I will separate nakedness, the necessity that we appear before God with the utmost honesty about ourselves, and the communion that that nakedness permits.

Nakedness

In Thomas Aquinas' treatment of prayer in the *Summa Theologiae*, he distinguishes two ways in which prayer unites us with God by the work of charity or love. The first is as the object of our prayer: We pray to be united with God, to be united with his will now, and to be united to him in knowledge after our death. But the simpler and prior form of unity is simply the lifting up of the mind to God. Thomas quotes pseudo-Dionysius: "When we call upon God in our prayers, we unveil our mind in his presence."[35] What is the nature of this unveiling?

Upon entering into silence, the first thing we notice is our own noisy thoughts. This surprises us, going against the romance of silence we may have imagined to ourselves.

The 2005 art-house documentary *Into Great Silence* captures the silence of La Grande Chartreuse, the famous Carthusian monastery in France. The power of the film, like the silence of the monastery, is the power of restraint, of countervailing expectations. We are introduced to the monastery without professorial speeches, emotionally exaggerated dialogue, without car chases or gunfire or background music. The film, like the place, is silent. Our feelings are invited, rather than provoked or managed. Yet it hides a truth about monastic silence from its viewers: Our thoughts make a racket.

I discovered the secret of inner noise on my first silent retreat. I signed up for eight days on beautiful farmland in southern Ontario, criss-crossed with walking trails. I was to speak only to my retreat director, and to hear in addition only the daily liturgy. I thought I was looking at eight days of peace and sweet rest. Instead, my thoughts shouted, each interrupting the other, under an immense cloud of anxiety. It was so strenuous that I could barely sleep. I was forced to confront the brute fact that the noise of my life came from the inside, not from outside. I had thought that the events of daily life shaped my anxieties, but it turned out the other way around: My anxieties drove the events of my life.

Dorothy Day, too, found monastic silence disruptive. Believing that she was too busy, she moved into a Dominican convent on Long Island. She was disappointed. In her retreat diary, she wrote: "My mind like an idiot wanders, converses, debates, argues, flounders. If I get in 15 minutes of honest to God praying I'm doing well." Day returned to her chaotic Catholic Worker House for good, having given up on a quieter life.[36]

Day's judgment that the encounter with inner pandemonium is a failure to pray seems to me not right. Prayer is a revelation of our inner selves in truth. If we are to sit before God, we must do so as ourselves. The Dominican priest and writer Herbert McCabe points to this when he insists that in making petitions, we must pray for what we really want. We have trouble focusing on prayer because we are not honest with ourselves: We pretend to care about things we do not in fact care about. Our "distractions," on his view, are the incursions of our real desires. "The prayers of people on sinking ships are not troubled by distractions," McCabe observed. "They know what they want."[37]

We can, of course, be deluded about what we want, and a life of prayer is meant to help us to clarify ourselves. An example, albeit not exactly in the context of prayer, comes from the stories told in *The Island* (*Ostrov*) (2005), where desperate people seek the help of the monk and holy fool Anatoly, the protagonist in the film. Anatoly is a clairvoyant; like a prophet, he hears what is secret and hidden. One woman tells the monk that she has never recovered from the loss of her great love who was killed in the war. Anatoly tells her that the lover is in fact alive, living in Paris, and that he longs to see his long-ago beloved. She must sell everything and go to see him while she still can. The woman is shocked. "But I'd have to sell my livestock!" she exclaims. He is not her great love after all, as is revealed when she learns that he has persisted in being alive and making demands on her. To seek out knowledge of our motivations in prayer and solitude is to acknowledge our ongoing capacities to deceive ourselves, and to seek out the truth, rather than waiting for it to be revealed happenstance in ordinary life.

At Madonna House, I practiced a form of prayer known as *poustinia*, the Russian word for desert. A poustinia is a small cabin or room in a house, sparsely furnished, where one goes for twenty-four hours to fast and pray, with only a loaf of bread, a jug of water, and a Bible. There too, inner noise dominates: Obsessive thoughts of one kind or another rush back and forth. But I found it could wear itself out, exhaust itself, over the course of twenty-four hours. It was also simply too long a time to maintain a pious performance for oneself, praying all hundred-fifty psalms, praying an entire rosary on one's knees. At some point, I would have to face myself, what I actually felt, what I actually wanted, and only then could I rest.

I learned how to drive as an adult and shortly thereafter sideswiped a van on a busy highway. I was changing lanes without looking. The van was only scratched – but the risk I had put the driver in was real, and the fault entirely mine. I pulled over behind the van. The driver stepped out, cursing and shouting. Somehow I had heard I wasn't supposed to say anything under these circumstances. So I didn't. I didn't apologize. I didn't explain. I listened, and I looked silently at the vehicles and their damage. I watched in awe as his anger ran out, like a balloon releasing pressurized air. He stopped shouting. We had a short conversation, where he suggested that we not go through the insurance companies. He contacted me later to ask for a bit of money for his trouble. I sent it. We were friends. My silence had somehow absorbed and exhausted his anger.

Our anxious thoughts and obsessions look for outlets in the world, reinforcement from words or actions of others. In silence and solitude, they run out of fuel, leaving emptiness, fatigue, openness, peace, or receptivity. Prayer unearths what one cares about most, whatever it is. In my experience, I am first revealed in the stupidity, vanity, or triviality of my inner monologue, which loses power the longer it is exposed without engaging with something or someone in the world. I catch a glimpse of my longing for God, which surprises me every time it comes to the surface.

The turning away from one's own stupidity and toward God is the movement of Christian repentance. Perhaps the most famous and beautiful of all the psalms is Psalm 51, where, by tradition, David repents of his theft of his wife Bathsheba and the murder of her husband. "Create in me a pure heart," the psalmist cries. He echoes the promise in Ezekiel that God will remove our stony hearts and replace them with hearts of flesh; or in Jeremiah, that the Israelites "shall return to [God] with their whole heart."[38] The exposure of one's "broken and contrite heart" is not punishment or humiliation for its own sake so much as it is a means of healing: This is the way hearts are created.[39]

Pious Delusions

The mystical writer John of the Cross praises the "knowledge of self" that emerges in the "darkness" of the soul, that is, when consolations are denied.[40] In silence and solitude, I discover what I really want and who I really am. I will be stripped of illusions that the competition and distraction typical of social life generate. Yet turning to God by entering a monastery and choosing silence, solitude, and fasting in no way guarantees to reveal ourselves as we are in truth. Before St. John turns to his famous writing on the highest forms of love and communion, he takes on the pious pretenses of novices. These beginners face the seven deadly sins, only with pious activity taking the place of their more typical objects, wealth, sex, conventional honors and prizes.

Consider spiritual anger, where the beginner "angry over the sins of others, reproves these others ... setting themselves up as lords of virtue."[41] Or spiritual gluttons, who seek after spiritual feelings and experiences, piling on liturgies, penances, and multitudes of books.[42] Those taken by spiritual avarice bejewel themselves in beautiful rosaries, holy cards, crosses, and icons, fussing over the perfect sign of devotion.[43] Or consider spiritual envy, where someone else's holiness is grounds for resentment, rather than gratitude or appreciation.[44] Most serious is spiritual pride, where one judges one's own spiritual condition to be under one's control, determined by the approval of others, by pious performances, or where a good relation toward God is thought to be found by condemning the faults of others. Instead of self-knowledge baptized in repentance and gratitude, pride drives a sense of urgency that God remove one's imperfections. After all, one was supposed to be perfect.[45]

One of the great literary examples of pride is Scobie, the central character of Graham Greene's *The Heart of the Matter*, who loses God after years of valiantly striving to protect his wife from his own adulterous affair.[46] More extensive and disturbing is the epic pride of Olav Audunssøn of Sigrid Undset's *Master of Hestviken*, who spends his entire life trying to undo the impact of a murder he committed secretly in his youth. His efforts only launch both him and his family deeper and deeper into catastrophe.[47] What is striking about both of these stories is the visible goodness in the character of each, their earnest

concern for others, and their willingness to sacrifice themselves – on their own terms – to reduce the impact of their
bad behavior on those they love. Pride, like all forms of
self-regard and striving to replace true humanity with fake
godlikeness, hides underneath even our best motives and
wrecks our best intentions.

If one is a convert, as I am, or if one has spent any
time around people who practice a religion, reading through
the literary accounts of pride or John of the Cross' catalog of
spiritual vice brings the crushing shame of self-recognition.
One begins to wonder whether anyone lives a true faith, if
any believer is truly humble and abandoned to God's will
for them. It is that sense of widespread inauthenticity and
lukewarmness that drives many into religious life, searching
for the real thing. In general, I believe they find it. The
disciplines of religious life are not either necessary or sufficient: one can be holy without them. Moreover, as we have
just seen, they provide no guarantees against our capacities
to deceive ourselves. Yet I hope it is becoming plausible that
the disciplines are often effective – all one can say of any
form of education or training.

Intimacy

What drew Catherine of Siena into the little closet in her
parents' house that served as her cell? It was there that she
consummated her mystical marriage to Christ. This intimacy might be explored through a way of life in some ways
more radical even than Catherine's was: the vocation of the
anchorite.

The eleventh to fourteenth centuries in England were the high-water mark of the anchorite movement. Men and women – it seems, especially women – from all walks of life discerned the vocation of the anchorite and walled themselves into a cell attached to a church. Unlike rural hermits, they lived in a village or town; unlike more flexible forms of solitary life, they were expected to live their whole lives in their cells, even unto death. Such a life was imagined as a crucifixion and a death, but also a kind of marriage. The author of the *Ancrene Wisse*, a rule of life for anchoresses from the early thirteenth century, writes:

> Understand, anchoress, whose spouse you are, and how he is jealous of all your doings . . . For this reason, he says in the *Canticles* [the Song of Songs 2:14]: *Ostende michi fatiem tuam* – "Show your face to me," he says, "and to no one else; look at me if you have clear sight with your heart's eyes. Look within where I am and do not seek me outside your heart. I am a bashful lover, I will not embrace my lover anywhere but in a secret place." In this way our Lord speaks to his spouse. Let it never seem strange to her if he shuns her if she is not much alone – and so much alone that she puts all the thronging world and every earthly disturbance out of her heart. For she is God's chamber.[48]

It is the intimate union with Christ, in prayer and in the Eucharist, present in the church on the other side of the wall, that draws in the anchoress, not love of suffering as such or hope of joy after death.

We should expect that the consummation of any love be a source of joy in itself. Another anchoritic work advises the anchoresses: "You will find such sweetness in his love and his service, and have so much joy of it and pleasure in your heart, that you would not wish to change the state in which you lived to be a queen."[49] How can we characterize this sweetness, which after all, should be the culmination of the types of life we are examining?

So austere a writer as Thomas Aquinas finds tender words to describe the intimacy with God in prayer: "When we pray to God, the very prayer we send forth makes us intimate with him, inasmuch as our soul is raised up to God and converses with him in spiritual affection, and adores him in spirit and in truth."[50]

The best way I know to communicate this affection, adoration, and mutual tenderness is through the writings of the fourteenth-century anchoress Julian of Norwich. Julian received a number of visions which she communicated in her book, *Revelations of Divine Love*. The writing is remarkable not just for the visions themselves, but for the warmth and gentleness of her tone. She writes,

> We know he shall appear suddenly and blissfully to all his lovers. For his working is privy, and he willeth to be perceived; and his appearing shall be sweet and sudden; and he will be trusted. For he is full kind and homely: blessed be he![51]

Julian is no pious idiot or sentimental fantasist, mouthing words without understanding. She is gripped by the question of how God can tolerate suffering and evil. More to the point, she is gripped by God's apparent absence, especially those who pray to him and seek his help. Through her revelations, she receives an insight:

> The continual seeking of the soul pleaseth God full
> greatly: for it may do no more than seek, suffer, and
> trust. ... The seeking, with faith, hope, and charity,
> pleaseth the Lord, and the finding pleaseth the soul and
> fulfilleth it with joy. And thus I was learned, to mine
> understanding, that seeking was as good as beholding, for
> the time he will suffer the soul to be in travail.[52]

Here Julian foreshadows John of the Cross. John argued that
the highest union with God in mortal life is found without
any consolation whatsoever, not even spiritual consolation,
in the dark night of the soul. Since God is transcendent,
unable to be touched or seen, one of our chief ways to know
him is through our longing for him. In darkness, John
thought, our desire would intensify, as for an absent, ill or
departed lover. The love of Mary Magdalene is his central
example. She ignores the prominent people at the banquet to
weep over Christ's feet.[53] John of the Cross writes:

> Such is the inebriation and the courage of love: Knowing
> that her Beloved was shut up in the tomb by a huge
> sealed rock and surrounded by guards so that his
> disciples could not steal his body, she did not permit this
> to keep her from going out with ointments before
> daybreak, to anoint him.[54]

It is in this passage that one can almost see how, in Julian's
terms, "seeking is as good as beholding." The intensity of
Mary's love is the same whether her love is present, absent,
alive, or dead.

For Julian, intimacy with God is union with him in
prayer, union with his will. Prayer does not change God's

mind but changes us so that we receive whatever happens as something good, as a gift for us personally.[55]

> Prayer oneth the soul to God. For though the soul be ever like to God in kind and substance, restored by grace, it is often unlike in condition, by sin on man's part. Then is prayer a witness that the soul willeth as God willeth; and it comforteth the conscience and enableth man to grace ... For he beholdeth us in love and would make us partners of his good deed, and therefore he stirreth us to prayer for that which it liketh him to do.[56]

In prayer, then, lies communion between the human lover and the divine beloved.

The Transformation of Experience

As Julian confronts the evils of the world in prayer, the Lord in her visions famously responds:

> All shall be well, and all shall be well, and all manner of thing shall be well.[57]

Such an insight suggests that communion with God, once experienced, is not confined to the solitude of the cell or the hermitage. A human marriage can allow the love of another person to infuse one's life, both in humble details of food and housing, and by providing a sense of the goodness of the world. Dante falls in love with Beatrice, and with God; when Beatrice dies, God is less interesting, and his life gradually declines so that the "way is lost."[58] Yet all human relationships must come to an end, and as crucial to our happiness as a particular person may be, the cause of goodness in the world is not any single individual. Once one acquires the habit of intimacy with God, all things and experiences can be taken in as goods, as gifts from the omnipotent ruler of everything.

The Danish philosopher Kierkegaard contrasted the movement of infinite resignation with the movement of faith, in part in terms of the transformation of experience. What he calls "infinite resignation" I have called "total renunciation": the withdrawal of the will from all that is not God, or that does not tend to the honor of God. It, too, is an act of love: Kierkegaard's image is of a lover sacrificing all, even the consummation of his love, for love of a princess. But infinite resignation is not the pinnacle of spiritual life; it is exceeded by faith. The man of faith, who finds himself in this condition by grace alone, receives back "the finite," all of the worldly things he initially renounced. He receives back everything he has sacrificed with joy, as a gift.[59]

The pilgrim narrator of *The Way of a Pilgrim* describes his experiences over a number of years, once he has undertaken the challenge of praying at all times. He learns to "pray with the heart," repeating the prayer called the Jesus prayer until it "somehow enters the heart itself."[60] He then describes the effects:

> When I began to pray with the heart, everything around me became transformed and I saw it in a new and beautiful way. The trees, the grass the earth, the air, the light, and everything seemed to be saying to me that it exists to witness to God's love for man and that it prays and sings of God's glory.[61]

Perhaps the pilgrim seems a fanciful character, from a very different culture than ours. Still, his tone strongly resembles that of twentieth-century writer Etty Hillesum. Hillesum's writing consists of a diary from the Nazi-occupied Netherlands, followed by letters written during the ten months she spent in Westerbork, a Nazi internment camp where she awaited deportation to Auschwitz.

Hillesum is matter-of-fact about her circumstances, but with unbreakable objectivity notices the beauty of skies and scenes, and she studies and reflects in faith on words of the scriptures. Lying sick with dysentery in the Westerbork infirmary, she wrote:

> Now and then I join the gulls. In their movements through the great cloudy skies one suspects laws, eternal laws of another order than the laws we humans make. This afternoon, Jopie, who feels thoroughly sick and all in, stood together with [me] for at least a quarter of an hour looking up at one of these black-and-silver birds as it moved among the massive deep-blue rain clouds.[62]

Hillesum's lightness of heart, her warmth, and her sense of wonder rival Julian of Norwich in their simplicity, and in the darkness lying in their background. Again, Hillesum is not simply deluding or distracting herself – she seeks to take everything in at once. From an earlier letter:

> A guard with an enraptured expression is picking purple lupins, his gun dangling on his back. When I look to the left I see billowing white smoke and hear the puffing of the locomotive. The people have already been loaded

onto freight cars; the doors are closed ... The sky is full of birds, the purple lupins stand up so regally and peacefully, two little old women have sat down on the box for a chat, the sun is shining on my face – and right before our eyes, mass murder. The whole thing is simply beyond comprehension.[63]

Hillesum simply takes in everything she sees, the tender beauty along with the horror, and lays the mystery up in her heart. She has found her way to this way of experiencing the world through what you might call an ordinary faith, lived in the world. She is not a nun. Yet she communicates the same thing that Mother Maria Sbotsova related after devoting herself to serving refugees: that "the whole of life becomes illumined."

We have seen that intimacy with God begins with the stripping away of illusions about oneself, and that it culminates in an experience of the loving presence of God. The sense of loving presence leads to the transformation of everyday experience. These movements form the core of Christian spiritual life in general, and religious life in particular. Yet that transformation is perhaps seen more clearly when we look at the other aspect of the virtue of charity, the love of one's neighbor as oneself. We turn there in the next chapter.

4   The Family of Humanity

T he Christian commandment to love follows first the words of Deuteronomy, that we are to love God "with all our heart, all our soul, and all our strength," and then the words of Leviticus, that we must love our neighbor as ourself.[1] Anchorites, hermits, and Carthusian monks and nuns, the religious who live in solitude, express their love of neighbor chiefly through prayer, as well as counsel to those who seek guidance from them. But most religious live in communities, where love of neighbor can be lived out in daily life.

Community, like solitude, is meant to be a school of love and a place of intimacy with divine love. Certainly, life at Madonna House, while punctuated by times of solitude in the little cabins called poustinias, was very much a communal life. We lived in dormitories, worked in groups, and shared meals together. Indeed, the constant presence of other people was so intense that my longtime extroverted character was forced inward. While once I found other people a regular source of excitement and energy, ever since I lived in a Christian community, I find groups wearing, and treasure solitude more than I ever did. That is because I learned to see social life as a place where the arduous work of love is practiced, rather than a sort of candy store for the attention and approval I crave by nature.

Earlier, we considered the call to religious life as a response to the ever-present prospect of death and annihilation, the fact that everything comes to an end, while our hearts long for eternity. God is sought as eternal and transcendent, in silence and solitude. Yet charity is a single and undivided condition of a person, with two aspects; Catherine Doherty described its structure as cruciform, vertically touching God, horizontally touching neighbor.[2] The collapse of human desire against life, then, may manifest not only as a love for God, but as the love of others, the love of humanity.

In the first chapter, we met Mother Maria Skobtsova, who became a nun after the death of her infant daughter, Nastia. She writes:

> For years I did not know, in fact I never knew the meaning of repentance, but now I am aghast at my own insignificance. At Nastia's side I feel that my soul has meandered down back alleys all my life. And now I want an authentic and purified road, not out of faith in life, but in order to justify, understand, and accept death. No amount of thought will ever result with any greater formulation than the three words, Love one another, so long as it is love to the end and without exceptions. And then the whole of life is illumined, which is otherwise an abomination and a burden.[3]

For Skobtsova, the encounter with death provokes self-knowledge, knowledge of what and who one is, and so a movement of repentance. The commandment to love one another then illuminates "the whole of life." Intimacy with God through loving others transforms her experience and consoles her in her grief. Loving others, however, is undertaken in a special way: "to the end and without exception."

Christian charity is not the love we feel for the likable, the charming, the good-looking, the powerful, or for those with whom we have a personal affinity. It is love for each human being, without exception and without condition. What does this love look like in practice?

The Unity of Humankind

The spiritual writer Caryll Houselander writes of her time in an English Catholic boarding school during the First World War. All of the nuns but one are French or Belgian, and the school is taken up into wartime fervor, including hatred of all things German. The other nun turns out to be Bavarian, with poor language ability in English or French, and without personal charm to draw others to her. One day Caryll sees her by herself in the shoe closet cleaning shoes. As she reaches to help, she notices that the nun is weeping, and she looks up to see a crown of thorns pressing down on the Bavarian sister's head.[4]

My readers are permitted to be skeptical of mystical visions like this one. Yet even if it were a fairy tale, it would help us to understand the transformation of experience that takes place through the Christian love of neighbor. In the course of ordinary life, human beings are divided from one another into rich and poor, resident or outsider, sick and healthy, enemy and friend. Through Caryll's pity for the "enemy" nun, she sees her as an image of Christ, and so sees Christ as uniting us, each with the other, through his suffering.

The promise of Christian community, of unconditional love universally practiced, is a community that looks like humanity, as described in the book of Revelation:

> After this I had a vision of a great multitude, which no
> one could count, from every nation, race, people, and
> tongue. They stood before the throne and before the
> Lamb, wearing white robes and holding palm branches in
> their hands.[5]

The heavenly community to come can be seen in visible
signs among communities in this world. Consider the beautiful description of the final community founded by Mother
Walatta Petros:

> Many women of high rank – daughters of princesses,
> concubines of the king, and the wives of great lords –
> were with Walatta Petros and took part in [her] work,
> following her. On one occasion, they would draw water,
> on another carry mud and stones. There were also many
> monks. Furthermore, there were those who had left
> father and mother, or wife and children, or all their
> possessions and fields, while others had sacrificed their
> youth and all their carnal desires. There were also women
> who had left their husbands, and virgins who had
> preserved their virginity and betrothed themselves to
> their groom Christ ... There further were children, boys
> and girls, who had followed their mothers. There were
> manservants and maidservants who had followed their
> masters, thereby liberating themselves from servitude,
> freeing themselves from subjection and becoming equal
> with their masters ... There were sinners and fornicators
> who had turned toward repentance, abandoning their
> former conduct and becoming virgins for Christ. And
> finally, there were poor and wretched folks, the blind and
> the lame: they had entrusted themselves to Walatta
> Petros and found refuge with her.[6]

Here is the pinnacle of Christian communal life, in the form in which it touches our hearts: all kinds of people, living as one family, with one set of common interests.

To live in such a community is as strict a form of self-denial as living in a remote hermitage without running water. The loving unity of all humanity, lived out in practice, makes war on our natural attachments. There is natural antipathy between the rich and the poor, slaves and masters, rule-followers and sinners, the able-bodied and those with disabilities. That is all before differences in manners and culture, habit and character, taste and humor, mode of work and leisure are taken into account. To love one's neighbor, then, requires the sacrifice of one's natural affinities with others, not only the bonds of contrived social exclusion, but the deep bonds of common affinity.

Other Monks

The actor Alec Guinness relates an exchange he once had on a visit to a monastery, prior to his formal conversion to Catholicism. A monk asks him, "What do you think is the greatest difficulty in the life of a monk?" Guinness promptly replied, "Other monks." The monk solemnly affirmed his answer.[7]

While preparing to enter Madonna House, I came across an address from a superior of the Dominican friars to a group of novices who had just taken the habit. "Take no consolation from the brethren!" he warned. "Your consolation must be from God alone." The words chilled me to the bone. What did it mean, not to take consolation from one's fellow novices? Was I setting out on a life without friendship or fellow feeling?

We think that love is a preference, and that such preferences are not only not harmful but open up to us the highest goods of life. But we know, in other contexts, that our preferences are hazardous. We prefer the good looking, the witty, the charming, the fully abled, those of our skin color, social class, and religion. Yet we muddle our thinking so that we don't see the obvious fact that such preferences are simply incompatible with loving one another on account of our simple humanity. Charity – the love of simple humanity, love of God, and love of neighbor – is the highest end of Christian life on earth. It is beautiful, but it makes constant war with our comforts.

The traditional monastic rule against particular friendship is the great bogeyman of the cinematic representation of religious life. Who can forget, once seen, the dreadful episode in *A Nun's Story* (1959), where the nun befriended by the protagonist confesses their attachment in the chapter of faults, and both are asked to scrub the floor in atonement? What could be more inhumane than a ban on human warmth and connection?

In truth it is not difficult to see how a preferential attachment might harm the common good. Consider the sign of peace congregants give one another at typical Catholic liturgies. What might be a moment of communion with the stranger and reconciliation with one's enemy becomes an opportunity for a tender smooch between happy couples, as the grieving and the lonely, those who have come to church seeking consolation, look around awkwardly.

At ordinary social gatherings, think of the best friends who speak a private language when others are trying to engage, or the couple so wrapped up in one another neither can connect with anyone else. We have all tried to have a conversation with the person whose children or pets are the only topics of interest; nothing and no one else seems visible to them.

I first came to Madonna House as a guest, for two stays of a couple of weeks each. Its hospitality guidelines discourage asking guests personal questions. No one knew that I was a philosophy professor. Even after I joined the community, it was not widely known that I had been trained as a teacher and a scholar. It was for me enormously liberating. I could suddenly see, through the eyes of others, who I was as a human being. Instead of traveling under the banner of "person of superior education," faced with the anxiety and exaggerated deference such a status inspires, I became one person among others. It turned out that I am a person with sparkling eyes, with a gift for small kindnesses and efficient work, prone to scold and to complain, with a sarcastic mouth and a fierce and unpredictable temper.

I had a conversation with a longtime member of the community during one of my first visits. "Madonna House is great," he said. "But I don't like *myself* at Madonna House." I learned to see that life with unchosen strangers laid bare one's own faults so that one lives with a painful self-consciousness, regularly realized if not constant.

In a religious community, one does not choose one's companions. Of all the sacrifices, for me that one had the most excruciating impact on daily life. The other guests are other recipients of hospitality, not necessarily fellow travelers. The fellow novices (or applicants as we were called) are not chosen for their common interests but according to their call to the community. The people one works with are determined by the various counterbalanced needs of the community, not personal compatibility.

One of the great shocks to me of entering the community was how fine-tuned my social preferences were. I had many friends; I prided myself on their political and religious diversity. But they were all bookish, and all middle class. How could I connect with people that fell into neither category? I was private and sarcastic; others were open and earnest. I hated consensus on principle and opted to be contrary; others did not understand contrariety in the face of the deepest truths of life. I found arguments entertaining; others found them rude or threatening.

The community, of course, is united in a common goal: love of God and love of neighbor. But unlike a knitting club, a polo club, a graduate program in philosophy, or a soup kitchen, that goal made no finer distinctions. I lived with people from various backgrounds and walks of life, in a community that looked more like humanity than any other group I have been in. It was wonderful, profound, and totally exhausting.

Among the forms of human speech sacrificed in common life are gossip, trivial comments about the lives of others: complaints, hasty judgments, salacious stories, speculations, cruel entertainments, and gratuitous criticism. When I was living in the community, to restrict my speech in this way did not come naturally to me. The impulse to relate an annoyance, a discovered secret, a joke at another's expense, for me is by default very strong.

For much of my youth, social anxiety fueled my social attachments. I had been a strange and abrasive child, and was often shunned or excluded by my peers. Once I found a way in (not until college), I was fearful of losing my place. So I located myself in anxious, exclusive groups, who ruthlessly put down or mocked outsiders. Such speech flatters the insider with inclusion while holding oneself up as a gatekeeper. It holds an implicit threat to exclusion also, should the insider act in the manner mocked or criticized. The grounds for exclusion may have been presumptively noble: We were, perhaps, intelligent, wise, authentic, morally upright, or edgy. Perhaps we drank fresh-brewed coffee rather than instant, read books rather than watched movies, or had in other respects excellent taste in consumer products. Nonetheless, such garden-variety exclusion is the antithesis of unconditional love.

The shortest path to a human connection is to draw someone aside and to distinguish the two of us as superior to others. If we avoid gossip and backbiting, especially when aided by a communal commitment to do so, we are cut off from this costly shortcut. One can only travel the long way into the heart of another: the slow work of finding common ground, the careful discernment of grounds for admiration, the disciplines of kindness, encouragement, silence, and restraint.

Selective control over our social lives need not be selfish, focused on the pleasures of exclusion or the joys of real affinity. There are other benefits. We choose to develop our interests, for our own good and the common good, with others: We volunteer for the maintenance of public parks, play cards, support local Democrats, ride motorcycles, or collect antique photography equipment. For the young, intense friendship is a means to escape the unchosen relationships of one's family of origin, to find unconditional love one might have been refused earlier, or to develop parts of oneself that might not develop otherwise.

Yet selective commitments cannot constitute the whole of social life, or we will find ourselves in a frenzy to replace friends whose affinity with us has been worn away by time or circumstances. The habits and pleasures formed by exercising social preferences can run onto rough shoals in any common endeavor with a variety of unchosen stakeholders. Social preferences may help to shape a marriage initially, but they will not sustain a commitment when the person you once chose in deep affinity proves rich, complex, and prone to change over time. The pleasures of chosen relationships may collapse in the face of one's children, who stubbornly insist on characteristics and behavior that you did not choose and cannot influence, even if they have the advantage of shared genetic material and shared domestic experience.

One's chosen friends also change as one's scope and path of life change. The fact is that our chosen relationships are hard to keep. Outside of chance, habit, fear, shame, or a safe distance, only unconditional devotion will maintain them. In the course of the ordinary changes a person undergoes in life, one's dearest friend, to whom one is unconditionally devoted, may end up further off in terms of affinity than many one might have scorned to befriend initially.

A deliberate choice, once and for all, renewed regularly, to love every human being one encounters saves us from the absurdity of clinging to something that in the course of things cannot be preserved.

The limits of human affinity can be illustrated by the limits of human agreement. Thomas Aquinas writes of peace as the fruit of charity. When we choose to will what God wills, and to love our neighbors as ourselves, "we wish to fulfill our neighbor's will as though it were ours."[8] Such a wish is a uniting of wills, not necessarily a meeting of minds.

Consider the common endeavors of building a house or working through a text in a seminar room. The unity is in a single shared desire, whose object may be articulated in various ways by various participants. It is the commitment to action that brings us together, despite all of our disagreements, practical, theoretical, trivial, or significant. Peace and charity are compatible with differences in opinion, not least because, as Thomas puts it, opinion is in the intellect and charity is in the will in action. In fact, in the most painful disagreements, one's underlying commitment to the other becomes more clear and more luminous.

In the book of Job, Job's bitter complaints invite a response from God himself, who speaks to Job out of the whirlwind. Job has complained that God is both all-powerful and impossible to understand; God in his response seems to affirm his view, without justifying or explaining himself. And yet Job is transformed by the interaction. It might seem so simply because of the act of communication, not because of any verbal or psychological agreement. God pays attention to him, holds him in mind, speaks to him, and shares his vision of the world with him. That means more than any answer to the question.

Love in community can be just as thin a reed, and just as profound. At Madonna House I fought great battles with my superiors. We would end up at loggerheads: They wanted something I couldn't give; I wanted something they wouldn't give. In the conflict, it would become clear that neither of us could give in – a change or even a compromise was simply not available. An open conversation would provide no resolution, but it did result in a kind of communion. I remember noticing how hard the other was trying to make things work. The effort touched me and affected me, likely more than their giving in to my preference would have done. It was in one way the most painful sacrifice, to give up persuasive communication on a matter you care about, and yet I walked away with a strange sense of peace and awe. No matter how passionate the disagreement, both parties in the commitment cared more about loving one another, living in peace and concord.

Celibacy

It might be noticed that in the course of ordinary life we sometimes sacrifice our ordinary affinities and social relationships, even those with our own family of origin. We do so, however, not out of love for God and neighbor, but for the love of one particular human being. The great rival to the choice of religious life – what most often tortures those in the process of discerning a vocation and those in early stages of formation – is erotic or romantic love. Celibacy, above all, repulses us from the religious life. When I was preparing to enter Madonna House, many friends raised concerns over the sacrifice of my career, the prospect of losing my personality in a cult, the separation it required from my friends and family. One college friend, famous for bluntness, was more frank. Her nose wrinkled: "Um ... *celibacy?*"

Our social relations can be mechanisms for a double life. We gather with others in strength to despise the weakness of others, pretending that we ourselves are not weak. We seek victory in social standing, pretending that our worth and dignity is somehow the product of our own hard work and merit, rather than luck or grace. Our perceived superiority to others hides us from knowledge of who we really are, fragile, vulnerable, and naked. Eve eats the fruit after the snake belittles her and persuades her that God, too, wishes to belittle her. Her desire to strive for social advantage and avoid disadvantage is her weak spot.

One might think that the fragility, vulnerability, and nakedness essential to erotic or romantic relationships might evade the trap of self-deception and the double life. Such evasion is possible, but its opposite may be more likely. A certain kind of intimacy with other humans, romantic partners, or parents, for that matter, can and does help us to know ourselves, to repent, to love and appreciate, to receive in gratitude. But such intimacy is not automatic. Christians are sometimes charged with being overly obsessed with sexual sins. There is truth in the charge: Failures in chastity, common in the world, are nothing next to the sin of pride, common in religious life. But the fact is that our sexuality can be a source of great harm toward ourselves and others, the root of violence, selfishness, an engine of illusion and delusion.[9]

In Eugene Voladzhin's novel of medieval Russian religious life, *Laurus*, the protagonist is born into grief. Both parents die of the plague when he is a child.[10] He is raised by his grandfather, an apothecary and healer, and trained in his profession. When he is a young man, his grandfather, too, dies, leaving him entirely alone and devastated by sadness. In his grief, a homeless young woman appears nearby, in need of healing. He heals her and falls in love with her. Their love is intense and profound but, on his part, characterized by extreme possessiveness. He hides her from the village, keeping her in a back room when villagers come to seek his advice. She becomes pregnant, but since marriage would require exposure to the public, he refuses it. She asks for a priest before giving birth, but he refuses it. She and her baby die in childbirth. His grief sends him over the deep end. He locks his door, staying with the rotting bodies and his decomposing mind, until the villagers intervene, knocking the door down, exposing his grief and his shame.

The image of a young man locked in a room with the rotting bodies of his beloved and child is startling in its horror. Yet its extremity, it seems to me, clarifies something fundamental about human sexuality. Our sexuality expresses what we hide in public: vulnerability, of course, but also violence, strangeness, childishness, and magical thinking. If we lead a double life, chances are, one of those lives is our sex life. The secret lives of the undercover KGB agents of the television series *The Americans* are characterized less by their national and political allegiances than by their sexual habits. One of the endlessly fascinating features of advice columns is their revelation of these double lives: the successful young man married to a slender, athletic woman, but who is really only attracted to overweight women he calls "trashy"; the upstanding citizen in the midst of a torrid affair.

Catherine Doherty tells the story of a wealthy white woman in 1930s New York who, at a public lecture, expressed contempt for Catherine's work for interracial justice and called her "dirty" for working with the "dirty n——s." One Saturday night in Harlem Doherty saw the same woman, out on the town, hanging on the arm of a black man with whom she was evidently involved.[11] In the gallery of horrors that constitutes the American racial imagination, it goes both ways: In *Light in August*, William Faulkner describes a liberal abolitionist woman sexually obsessed with the supposed blackness of her light-skinned lover.[12] Our racial and class prejudices infuse our sexual desires, doling out attractiveness to some, denying it to others.[13]

We may know these people, or we may know others like them, with fantasies of vampire nuns or truckers dressed up like cheerleaders or whose sexual identity is a stuffed animal. These men and women walk among us, cool, calm, collected, and apparently completely normal. Prostitutes and sex workers see truths that none of us suspect. Who can forget the chilling scene in Orwell's *Down and Out in Paris and London* when the head of a bordello sends a man who has offered her a fortune for a prostitute "to go down into the cellar and do whatever he wants"?[14] Certain desires do not go out in public. To be expressed, they need utter privacy; if they involve other people, they involve the helpless and the vulnerable, the poor and dependent, the invisible ones. The spaces of brutal sexual exploitation are hidden from view, in respectable homes, it is true, but also in pockets of poverty, on the modern versions of the island of Emperor Tiberius, the destinations of sex tourists.

One need not judge private habits or wade into sexual ethics to see that the double lives I have described are incompatible with Christian wholeheartedness. But wholeheartedness, like the other Christian disciplines we have seen, is based in acts of will, not in passing feelings or occurrent thoughts. There is no reason to think that celibacy or sexual abstinence magically heals our sexual disorder, our dark realm of magical thinking and suppressed desire. Abstinence itself can become a get-out-of-jail-free card; under its pretenses, our disorders can hide behind a wall of denial, only to emerge without warning, at best betraying our integrity, if not causing damage in the form of real abuse.[15]

On this account, Christian life in general and religious life in particular require relentless self-examination and a habit of openness: sacramental confession for Catholics and Orthodox, a habit of communicating with one's abbot.[16] An honest confrontation of our sexuality, celibate, chaste or no, is necessary to live in the truth about oneself, even if, like the other truths of life, it is deeply humbling and uncomfortable to face.

Sexual desire cuts into the depths of our souls; success in love can give our life meaning, and failure ruthlessly put us in despair. That gives our sexuality urgency and importance, a natural centrality in human life. But its strength does not bring purity with it. It is susceptible to corruption by the other desires and ambitions, superficial as they seem, that can wreck human life. Indeed, this is as obvious as anything can be: Think of those who love violently, indifferently, dishonestly, carelessly, cruelly, or thoughtlessly.

I have been severe on sexuality, not out of prudishness, but to counter the overwhelming rhetoric on the other side. We act as if life without sex is impossible, and entertain the thought, even if less commonly nowadays than in my youth, that sex with strangers is harmless. Both cannot be true: Either sex reaches down to the core of our being, and so ought be treated with reverence and caution, as something which might bear life's meaning for us, or it is harmless, like chewing bubble gum, and can be given up without a second thought. The fact is that the depth and significance of our sexual desires make celibacy very difficult, but it is by no means impossible. Life without sex has been lived many times, in many walks of life, without grave harm of any kind.

Wholeheartedness is not reserved to celibacy alone; it is the true grandeur of romantic and sexual love. Even the main character of *Laurus*, who shows the ugliness of erotic love so clearly, loves his wife with true wholeheartedness, devoting his life to God in atonement for her death, keeping her always in loving attention. Such grandeur appears when the love for one person opens oneself up, exposes one's insides to another, the petty darknesses and the old wounds, and so frees oneself from fear of rejection. In its unconditional form, in its tenderness in the face of every obstacle, it is itself a school of charity. True intimacy cultivates freedom; freedom and wholeheartedness, like those sought in religious life, are the result of total commitment, of love without condition, without counting the cost.

Our most intense human relationships, between parents and children, or between romantic partners, rely on the pleasures of intimacy: mutual material dependence, fellow-feeling, extensive shared experience, the exposure of one's deepest wounds, the touch of body to body. One cannot experience this intensity with many people; it is by its nature reserved to a few. Such love is essential for most, perhaps all, of us, not because of its pleasures but because of the unique combination of deep exposure and deep acceptance. Our families see who we are. They have no illusions about us. And they love us anyway.

In the best cases then, a family or a marriage can be the same training ground for love of humanity that a religious community can be. That follows from the inevitable decay of the grounds for our affinity to one another; as life goes on, we are worn down from loving one another for entertainment, status, or comfort into the commitment to the person as such, as a human being worthy of love. Despite the sound of it, there is nothing cold about such a love. It is the love that shines through deprivation and suffering of all kinds, love "to the end and without exceptions," as Mother Maria Sbotsova puts it.

Loving Attention

I have spoken of the sacrifices involved in the love of one's neighbor in the religious life, the sacrifice of one's affinities with others, and the sacrifice of intimate attachment to a single person. So far then, I have said what is lost, but I have not said what is gained. Like the concentrated clarity about oneself that emerges in silence and solitude, community life also shifts and clarifies focus. Much of Christian asceticism the deliberate restriction of one's attention, of what one sees, hears, knows, and pays attention to, in the hope of an ever more simple focus on what really matters. The restriction of the senses, of the sense of sight and hearing especially, is for the sake of wholeheartedness. The wholehearted focus in a community is on others, and that takes place in two ways: through work and through prayer.

The English word charity is associated with "charitable endeavors": the care of the sick and the dying, the housing of refugees, the feeding of the hungry, and the clothing of the naked. Each human being has needs thanks to the character of our bodies: We require food, drink, clothing, and shelter; when we are sick or dying, we can do little for ourselves. Thanks to the difficulty of this work, it serves as a school of charity in much the same way that community life does. The sick, the dying, the homeless, the desperately poor may or may not be polite, gracious, well-groomed, and interesting conversationalists. Serving the poor acts against a default natural tendency, to avoid the sick and the suffering, to move the homeless out of sight, to cross the street when faced with someone of evident mental illness.

While the poor and needy make unusual requirements on us thanks to their circumstances, their needs as such are the same as ours. It is less evident, but every bit as true, that the wealthy also need others to help us fill our needs. In a small community, our mutual dependence on one another is simply more visible. That is especially so in a community like Madonna House, which grows much of its own food, and which builds, maintains, and cleans its own buildings. If a community member does not make dinner when expected, there will be no dinner; if they do not take out the trash, the room will stink – or someone else will have to do it. Whether one experiences mutual dependence in gratitude for the help one has received, or annoyance at how something is done or not done, either way, the reality of dependence is very obvious.

In ordinary non-communal life, I also depend on others to grow and prepare my food, to manufacture my cleaning materials, my clothing, and my medications; my shelter needs to be first built, then maintained . . . and so on. In contemporary life, those who do this work are invisible as often as not, and so the simple joy of giving another what they need is blunted, unseen, or lost entirely.

We have, moreover, developed forms of work that are completely disconnected from human needs. Consider the high-prestige, highly paid exercises in futility described by David Graeber in his book *Bullshit Jobs*. Men and women find themselves paid not to fix things that need to be fixed; to fix things in such a way that they will certainly break again; to look after reams of paperwork that are strictly necessary and that absolutely no one cares about. The papers go into files that are never, ever opened. The effect of these forms of work on the workers themselves, as Graeber describes it, is soul-destroying.[17]

The most humanly useful work, in our culture, is most despised: Cleaning bathrooms, collecting garbage, serving meals – all lie at the bottom of our social totem pole. We find it moving to hear of wealthy celebrities or officials who do their own cooking or their own shopping or their own laundry. It is a sign of their humanity, their recognition that a human community is and can be a web of loving service. Work in itself is for the good of others, a form of service. When done for love, the simplest work is an act of charity.

Intercession

I have mentioned the needs of the body, but of course we also need other things: comforting conversation when we are in distress; teaching when we do not know or understand; counsel as to what to do next; warning when we are in danger; and prayer, the loving attention given to the needs of others in light of our mutual dependence on God. The practice of intercession, praying for the needs of others, is central to any religious life, especially those in cloisters or hermitages. For enclosed communities, it is the way that the family of humanity is kept in view.

In intercessory prayer, prayer for others, the sick, the dying, the devastated, the grieving, the unjustly imprisoned, the victims of every crime and every injustice, everyone anywhere who suffers for any reason, all come into focus. It is an ascetic practice: the replacement of thoughts of oneself with thoughts of others, the sacrifice of one's one will and one's own concerns for God's sake. In the ordinary course of life, among the people one happens to know, family, co-workers, friends, sorrows and joys come with some regularity, sometimes clustered, sometimes apart, but inevitably they come. One's attention is drawn in for a time, then drawn away. The Christian practice of intercession focuses one's attention on the needs of others, strangers as well as friends, those known and unknown. The deliberate focus is a form of service, an invitation to hear the needs of others. So it is that every religious community, as well as every hermit, anchorite, or consecrated person, takes on intercession as a part of its work.

In Aelred of Rievaulx's instructions for anchoresses, he describes intercession as a form of almsgiving for those who have nothing:

> With pity behold him who is in disease, as poor people, destitution of widows, desperate souls, needs of pilgrims, perils of shipmen, vows of maidens, temptations of monks, cares of prelates, and labors of toiling people.[18]

It is sometimes charged against cloistered or enclosed religious that they hide themselves from the real world. The practice of intercession suggests rather that those who live in enclosure focus with greater intensity on the needs and suffering, joys and sorrows of others, at a far broader level than one might in the course of ordinary life in the world.

To get a sense of the breadth and depth of this practice, one can ask a religious community for its prayer list. One can also search Twitter for "please pray." Just now I found these: several babies in the hospital, undergoing major operations; a six-month-old infant killed by a dog; a woman in chemotherapy; a man paralyzed in an accident; four brothers, all children, abducted on their way to school; a dead parent; a dead nephew; a student overwhelmed by exams; a man suffering from depression and anxiety; a relative shot multiple times; a relative in grave moral danger; every form of death, every form of illness, every form of suffering. Alongside the sorrows are the new endeavors on which one wishes success: a new job, starting college, getting married, getting pregnant, entering religious life.

It is common to pray not just for individuals but for whole categories of suffering: for the sick or the grieving, for the oppressed and imprisoned, for orphans, widows, and catechumens, for travelers and for political leaders, for particular countries, for oppressed minorities, for justice in one area or another, for peace, for an end to war, for the conversion of the world to the pursuit of charity. Intercession is a chosen awareness of sorrows and difficulties, and an expression of hope that good comes from them, whether the hoped-for resolution, healing, justice, resurrection, or the strange consolations of the Christian, the lights in darkness.

The Transformation of Experience, Again

The life of solitude and communion with God alone that we saw in the previous chapter led to a transformation of everyday life: The smallest thing of goodness or beauty shines with divine glory. So too with a life of charity: In the darkest circumstances, amid the pain and suffering of others, the light of charity changes it.

Raymond of Capua describes an incident in the life of Catherine of Siena. Catherine was visiting a woman with breast cancer. The woman's cancer had formed an enormous, infected wound on her chest. Catherine's stomach turned at the foul smell. Catherine became angry at her natural reaction, which rebelled against her intention to find joy in the love of her neighbor. She forces her nose close to the wound and smells, miraculously, an incredible sweetness. In a similar incident with the same woman, a bucket of infected fluids reeks, provoking intense nausea and disgust. Catherine forces herself to drink it, and by a miraculous divine intervention, it tastes as sweet as nectar to her.[19]

Catherine acts against her instinct, mortifying her repugnance. Such "acting against," called by Ignatius *agere contra*, is central to Christian asceticism.[20] St. Thérèse, faced with a fellow nun whom she disliked intensely, forced herself to act against her sentiments. She treated the nun with unusual grace and kindness, "as if she were the person I loved best in the world." Her efforts were effective to the point that the nun came to believe that Thérèse was especially attached to her. In language echoing the experiences of Catherine and of Caryll Houselander, Thérèse remarks,

> Of course, what really attracted me about her was Jesus hidden in the depths of her soul; Jesus makes the bitterest mouthful taste sweet.[21]

————

My own experience was transformed while living at Madonna House, in ways I find more difficult to communicate. The main way I would put it is to say that while living there, it was impossible to waste time. Part of the power of religious life in community is its use of time. There are hours of prayer, work times, study times. Under obedience, little is left to personal whim. It permits an intense focus.

The idea that religious life is especially useful reverses a more obvious view of religious life: that it is a waste of one's time and talent. "What a waste," mutters the disappointed mother of a beautiful young woman taking the Benedictine habit, in the film version of Rumer Godden's *In This House of Brede*. She means that her beauty should be used to attract and keep a husband, and then to bear children as it fades. Articulated that way, everything may seem like a waste. "What a waste," mutters the poet Yeats, noting the degeneration of a brilliant friend to wife and mother.[22] The brilliant professor played by Emma Thompson in *Wit* (Mike Nichols, 2001) realizes as she loses a battle with cancer that it has all been a waste.

The voice of Solomon in Ecclesiastes claims that "The eye is not satisfied with seeing, nor the ear with hearing." We can't get enough of experiencing. We always want more. We see and hear as if we had indefinite time. What else could account for the appalling degree to which we waste our sensory experience? If we knew the finitude of our lives, really knew it, would we spend hours upon hours binge watching or obsessively reading the news? Would we gossip and speculate on matters that are no business of ours? Would we spend hours searching for skincare products or the perfect briefcase?

The fake busy-ness that is in fact a form of distraction is called by the ancient monks *acedia*.[23] It is listlessness or lack of joy in the most important things. It is the plague of modern middle-class life.

While a guest at Madonna House, trying out the life before entering their formal novitiate or training program,

I fell in love with the somber hymn that we sang every morning in Lent, in wintry Russian tones. "I have wasted my life in laziness!" the speaker pleads. He seeks the mercy of God to be useful, to be good. Another guest, who was preparing to join a community of friars who lived as poor men among the poor, spoke to me suddenly about his life, saying, "I've wasted so much time." I was struck, as I thought: In four months here, I haven't wasted any time.

It was true. My life was ordered to prayer and to acts of service, in virtue of working for the community, whether that was something as simple as sweeping or dishwashing or something as specialized as repairing books or furniture. Whether those acts of service were selfish or acts of charity is not something I could decide for myself: Like faith and hope, in Christian teaching, charity comes only by grace, by free gift, and it is known only to God. But knowing who was aided by the work I did, knowing what would happen if it were left undone, helped me to focus on those the work served. That is the point of a simple life, I think: transparency of purpose. When I had a bit of free time, I had no money to spend, no place to go, and the internet was off-limits. I walked in the woods, wrote letters, played cards, read books, had a conversation. It was a life of focus, without daily regret.

Neighbors and Enemies

Charity, the love of each and every human being, is not something anyone is born with. It is the product of formal or informal training, crowned with the grace of God. Yet to love our neighbors as ourselves, we must love ourselves; and we do not love ourselves without being loved. For many of us, that unconditional love, the love that sees every weakness and still treasures, is given by our parents or by another loving adult, in childhood. For others, we find it later in life, from a spouse or from no human being but thrown into the arms of God alone.

The 1975 made-for-television movie of Rumer Godden's novel *In This House of Brede* gives a lucid summary of the monastery as the school of love. Philippa Talbot, a successful London businesswoman, gives up her career and the man who loves her to become a Benedictine nun. She has lost her husband and child – both dearly loved; she has already given up a romantic friendship with a married man. In the convent she becomes passionately attached to a young postulant with the same name as her dead daughter. The postulant, Joanna, having left an emotionally frosty biological mother outside the monastery walls, returns her attachment.

The filmmaker never falls into the common folly of popular representations of the religious life. He does not treat the ban on particular friendships as a tyrannical suppression of human emotion but presents it as a prudent redirection of energy to loving each person without exclusion. It is obvious that the attachment these two women have to one another lies as an obstacle for each to a greater form of love.

What love could be greater than a mother's for her child, or the romantic friendship of two adults with some experience of the world? Love of neighbor might be sufficient, but the filmmaker takes us straight to the top, to the love of one's enemies. Philippa's enemy is Dame Agnes, the eternal "Sister Cranky" that we find whenever a nun makes an entrance on the silver screen. Dame Agnes argues against Philippa's admission to the monastery and against her final profession. Dame Agnes is rigid. Dame Agnes is jealous. Dame Agnes judges Philippa severely and tattles on her misdeeds to the abbess. In fact, it is Dame Agnes that tells the abbess that Dame Philippa and Joanna have been spending too much time together.

Dame Agnes supplants Dame Philippa in the novitiate. Phillppa, having given up her "daughter," seeks an emotional connection with the other nuns. She endeavors to work below her social class, scrubbing floors and cleaning bedpans in the infirmary. Dame Agnes collapses on the stairway from a heart attack. Agnes awakes at night to see Philippa praying at her bedside. She confesses her fault and asks forgiveness. It is granted. Dame Agnes dies in Philippa's arms.

I have my prejudices, but I think there is no more beautiful love scene in all of cinema than the deathbed reconciliation of these two nuns who have spent years in mutual hatred. Is it possible for us, our hearts crowded as they are with a million emotional demands, obligations, and impulses, to see the love of one's enemy, so simple and homely as this is, as the highest achievement of a human life?

If we do accept it, then I think we must ask the question that Christians have always asked: How is it possible? What about the monastery has been effective in its cultivation?

It is of course possible to love one's enemies without a monastic endeavor. Prince Andrei, the proud and brilliant protagonist of *War and Peace*, finds himself gravely wounded in a field hospital after the Battle of Borodino. Only steps away lies the callow playboy who seduced his fiancée. The one-time rival has lost his legs and is screaming in pain. The seduction of the fiancée, which has ruined Andrei's happiness, shrinks to a pinhole in the face of Anatole's pain and Andrei's own impending death. Andrei forgives him, along with his fiancée, effortlessly.

Nor is monastic life sufficient to instill love of enemies. Whatever the absurd distortions of the secular literature on monasticism, it is surely true that religious superiors have abused their power in cruelty and injustice, and even more true that many religious communities wallow in simple mediocrity, unwilling to risk severe cruelties, but likewise unwilling to break hearts for love as is necessary. If the abbess of Brede had not intervened, Philippa and Joanna would have clung to one another and have been blind to their deeper and greater possibilities.

Radical Forgiveness

The Beatitudes as they appear in Luke's Gospel bring out a connection between the blessings of suffering and the love of enemies. Matthew gives eight conditions for good fortune; Luke gives only four: poverty, hunger, sorrow, and persecution. In addition to the four conditions of blessedness, there are four conditions of disaster: wealth, satisfaction, laughter, and public praise. Poverty brings happiness; wealth brings woe. Immediately following, we find the exhortation to love one's enemies.

> Love thy enemies; do good to those who hate you, pray
> for those who mistreat you. To the person who strikes
> you on one cheek, offer the other, and from the person
> who takes your cloak, do not withhold even your tunic.[24]

The Sermon on the Mount in Matthew also contains the call
to love our enemies and to turn the other cheek. But the
proximity to the Beatitudes in Luke suggests a connection. If
our good fortune comes by poverty, hunger, mourning,
littleness, and persecution, how is it possible not to love
our enemies? Those who inflict these conditions on us have
only helped us.

The love of enemies is at once the most splendid
and the most challenging of the Gospel commandments. It
suggests an endorsement, a loving embrace even, of the
gross injustices of the world. Yet I think even its harshest
critics can be moved by it. The stories of true peacemaking,
rare as they are, where two murderous warlords recognize
each in the other and lay down their arms, can melt the
frostiest of hearts. I remember weeping in my second week
at college at the reconciliation between Achilles and Priam at
the end of the *Iliad*. Achilles has butchered half the army
and has dragged the corpse of Priam's son around his camp,
over and over again. At Priam's dignified request for the
body, and at his mention of his own father, Achilles cracks.
He gives the body back. His rage is broken.

Models of forgiveness are highly sought-after
speakers and authors: for example, Kim Phuc Phan Thi,
who forgave those who bombed her with napalm and those
who exploited her pain; or Immaculée Ilibagiza, who forgave

the man who slaughtered her family in the Rwandan genocide. In the United States, news stories of forgiveness for terrible crimes are eaten like candy, as when in 2006, the Amish forgave a man who shot ten girls at their school, or in 2015, when the relatives of those slain in church by white supremacist Dylann Roof express their forgiveness of the killer in court.[25]

The scandal is obvious. Victims of abuse and injustice are often taught and trained to deny their abuse, or to accept blame for it. Christian ideals are ready to be exploited by those to whom the anger of victims might be harmful, dangerous, or embarrassing. But a Christian ideal properly speaking must be undertaken in freedom, out of love. If we are to love our neighbors as ourselves – which surely comes before the love of enemies – we must love ourselves first and see ourselves as proper objects of love. The victim's avoidance of conflict and the self-hatred required for it has nothing Christian about it. The point is not that my enemy is better than me or that I deserve my ill treatment, but that God has worked through all events, rendering my enemy powerless over me. Moreover, in my life of inward scrutiny, honesty, and humility, I come to recognize the characteristics of the enemy in myself, and greater possibilities in him. We meet one another on the ground of our common humanity.

One's own suffering cannot be used for one's good, or accepted as from God, except by the active consent of the victim, out of love, in virtue of a personal relationship with a God who saves. The fact that the conquest of violence is possible can never, for this reason, excuse violence. Those who seek to justify violence lack the authority to conquer it in this way.

Josephine Bakhita, when asked at a gathering of students what she would do if she met her kidnappers, replied with the following:

> If I were to meet those who kidnapped me, and even those who tortured me, I would kneel and kiss their hands. For, if these things had not happened, I would not have been a Christian and a religious today.[26]

The words may be shocking, until we remember that she did not kiss the hands of her Italian masters and accept her position as a slave. On the contrary, she sought her freedom and got it. She used that freedom to reach for a different level of reality, where everything that happens to us can be a vehicle of grace. It is crucial to defy one's enemies, but the ultimate defiance is to take the sting out of their bite, to use what one receives from them for one's own good and the good of others. Kim Phuc Thanh Thi, writing openly about her decades of anger and bitterness, comes to a hard-won conclusion that echoes Bakhita: "Those bombs led me to Christ."[27] The point is *not* that there is no such thing as loss or no such thing as suffering, but, as Paul puts it, the gain of Christ makes all losses seem trivial. It is here where the Gospel parable of the man selling everything for a single pearl begins to come into view.

The injunction to love enemies, to turn the other cheek, or to offer the tunic along with the cloak to a robber can be seen as acts of defiance, as exercises of a profound freedom. Chesterton describes the way that Francis of Assisi casts light on the Gospel command as a kind of practical joke:

> There is in [the note of St. Francis] something of the gentle mockery of the very idea of possessions; something of a hope of disarming the enemy by generosity; something of a humorous sense of bewildering the worldly with the unexpected; something of the joy of carrying an enthusiastic conviction to a logical extreme.[28]

Once harm is seen as an instrument of God, the violent lose their power.

St. Lawrence, according to an old legend, was executed by the Romans in 258, roasted on a gridiron. From the fires of the gridiron, he cried out to his executioner: "Thou cursed wretch, thou hast roasted that one side, turn that other, and eat!"[29] The comic stance of Lawrence is seen in a loftier light by Leo I, commemorating him:

> You gain nothing, you prevail nothing, O savage cruelty. His mortal frame is released from your devices, and, when Laurentius departs to heaven, you are vanquished. The flame of Christ's love could not be overcome by your flames, and the fire which burnt outside was less keen than that which blazed within. You but served the martyr in your rage, O persecutor: you but swelled the reward in adding to the pain.[30]

Takashi Nagai, survivor of the bombing of Nagasaki, reflected especially on two stories. The nuns of Josei convent who had survived the initial blast, terribly burned, had been heard singing, clustered by a cool stream, as they died. Likewise, the young girls at the local school had been taught in the dark days of the war to sing a hymn every day for God's protection. Groups of these girls, with gruesome injuries, many of them dying, gathered in various shelters, would encourage one another by singing the hymn.[31] The singing martyr is stronger than the killer. The seeker of harm becomes the object of charity, revealed as a weak and powerless person rather than a strong one.

To say that violence or oppression does not harm the person who seeks holiness or union with God is neither an endorsement nor a justification of wrongdoing. From the perspective of the wrongdoer before God and the truth, deliberate harm is under a cloud of ignorance, selfishness, and malevolence. It leaves a human being isolated, fragmented, and prone to more delusions. The instinct to rationalize and ignore grows stronger proportionate to the work it must do to save appearances. In Christian moral teaching, nothing could be worse for a person than using power for injustice. Our fight against injustice is for the good of the persecutors and can be undertaken out of true love for them

The line between neighbors and enemies need not be bright, as the example from the fictional house of Brede shows. Those closest to us can do the most harm to us and to our projects. It is easy enough to avoid loving either neighbor or enemy; it is sufficient simply to keep one's distance. Only intimacy, with its stripping away of our illusions and the war it makes on our double-mindedness, permits us to love truly. Otherwise, we skate on the surfaces of things, seeking human connection by shortcuts, shifting interests, and a fleeting sense of superiority. Religious life is not the only way to cultivate the love of neighbors and enemies. Yet I think it is the most deliberate and effective way, the way freest from distractions, where that end can become the goal one strives for every day, with every action, with the support of those around you.

5   Abandonment and Freedom

The love of enemies requires the capacity to see one's sufferings as good, as successes or blessings. This kind of vision is an aspect of a broader condition, known as abandonment. In the state of abandonment, one accepts not only human wrongdoing as from the hands of a beloved enemy, but any disaster, natural or otherwise, as coming from the hand of God in his providence.[1] The state of abandonment is the end for which total renunciation is an effective means. But as we shall see – as perhaps we have already seen – vows, promises, and penances are neither necessary nor sufficient to achieve it.

We all face death at least once, and disaster at least sometimes, in illness, job-loss, heartbreak, hurricanes or earthquakes, as chance or providence doles out. Could it be, not only that we live most fully in the face of death and disaster, but that a fuller sort of life is available to us, if we choose, all at once, to give up everything?

So argued a brilliant nun who ran a boarding house in Washington, DC, where I lived for a time. She had worked in leper colonies in East Africa for most of her apostolic life. After a bout with cancer, she was sent to the USA for the more peaceful work of running a house full of women studying at the local Catholic institutes. She was the daughter of a well-respected doctor in her hometown in Colombia. She entered religion, despite a devoted fiancé, thinking that it was unlikely that she would be sent out of the country. Immediately upon entering she was sent abroad, never to return.

I stayed at the boarding house when I was preparing to go up to Madonna House to enter their formation program. I mentioned that I was "negotiating" how many books I could bring. Sister Martha was horrified. "Negotiating with the novitiate!" she cried. "What you don't give up, life takes from you."

We middle-class North Americans sometimes are unprepared for objectivity and receive it as severity. But Sister was dead right. Your treasured career is at the mercy of the market. You cling to your native land or your hometown and find yourself in an instant an exile or a refugee. You can put your marriage and children above everything and lose them anyway, to accident, disease, or something less than that. The only thing that you have a hope of not losing is God. Abandon yourself now, abandon yourself later – what difference does it make? The poet Gerard Manley Hopkins puts it more gently: "The thing we freely forfeit is kept with fonder a care / fonder a care kept than we could have kept it."[2]

Abandonment is the fulfillment of Christian life; its clearest examples, of which I shall relate three, must be the examples of Christian life that a secular non-believer will find most appalling.

Facing One's Own Weakness

Walter Ciszek was a Jesuit priest who felt called to travel into Communist Russia in order to minister to those living under a totalitarian regime where religion was outlawed. Unable to enter Russia in 1937, after he was ordained, he was sent instead to an Eastern Catholic parish in eastern Poland. In 1939, under the terms of the Hitler–Stalin pact, as Hitler invaded Poland from the west, the Russians poured in from the east, occupying Ciszek's town and the surrounding area. Russia had come to him.[3]

The Eastern-rite parish under Ciszek's care was harassed by the occupying soldiers and forced to close. He and another Jesuit priest trained for Russia received permission to investigate the conditions for ministry in Russia itself, among the work camps in the Ural Mountains. When Hitler invaded Russia in 1941, the two priests were betrayed, captured, and accused of spying on behalf of the Germans for the Vatican. Ciszek spent five years at the KGB prison Lubianka under interrogation and was finally sentenced to fifteen years in the labor camps in Siberia. Once freed to live in designated Siberian cities, he wrote to his family in the United States, who had presumed him dead. For eight years, they lobbied for his return, until he was released in 1963, thanks to a deal between the US and Soviet regimes.

Ciszek told the story of his long captivity in two remarkable books, the first telling the story in its broadest blow-by-blow outline, the second telling the same story in terms of the spiritual practices that he judged to have preserved his life and his sanity.

Ciszek was born in 1904, the son of Polish immigrants, his father a coal miner. In his youth, Ciszek tells us, he was a "tough," "a bully, a leader of a gang, a street fighter."[4] He was set back a grade by playing hooky, and his parents took him to the police station to insist he be sent to reform school. They were tender parents, on his account, but unable to understand why he did not take his education seriously. In eighth grade, he suddenly decided to be a priest. His father, seeing his utter lack of natural holiness, resisted, but finally agreed. For the rest of his schooling, his seminary training, and his training to be a Jesuit, he took on the hardest things, refusing to accept that he couldn't do anything that anyone else did. On his own account of himself, Walter Ciszek loved the impossible and mortified his loves for the sake of greater excellence and endurance.

It is against this background that he tells what to me is the most extraordinary story in an astonishing series of experiences. He has already been captured and has left the foul and crowded jails, where despite the fearful conditions, he finds solace with the political prisoners he has been captured with. He is taken to Lubianka, where the guards wear soft cloth shoes in order to maintain a deathly silence. He sees and hears no one and is fed little. His only interactions are with his interrogator.

Ciszek is not guilty of the charge of spying for the Vatican; the KGB already know his factual crime of entering Russia on a false passport. He assumes that eventually they too will figure out the truth. But he is worn down over months of isolation, by the psychological jujitsu of the interrogator, by hunger, and by the utter uselessness of telling the truth, over and over again. The interrogator drugs and tortures him, then returns under a kindly demeanor. He makes a confession, saying nothing but the truth.

The interrogator returns a "transcript" to him, filled with falsehoods, to be signed on each page. He hesitates. The interrogator, suddenly angry, threatens to execute him. In an exhausted panic, Ciszek gives in, signing page after page of a false confession.

As what he has done sinks in, that he has utterly failed to resist the KGB's machinations, he is overwhelmed with shame and darkness. He has given in to the enemy. All of his struggles have been for nothing. In the midst of that darkness, he comes to the epiphany that guides him through the next twenty years of brutal captivity. Why is he over-whelmed with guilt and shame? he wonders. He panicked, under the threat of violent death. In Catholic teaching, there is no sin without consent and no consent possible under threat of violence. He is blameless.

He sees that his previous expectation that he could endure the interrogations was simply pride. He has prayed and worshipped in pious noises, while reserving thoughts of his own excellence and his superior abilities to endure. He has relied on himself, rather than on God. In the end, he has proved merely human, unworthy of trust.

"Put no trust in princes, in mortal men in whom there is no help,"[5] the psalmist says, and elsewhere, "A vain hope for safety is the horse; despite its power, it cannot save." No human resource has sufficient power to overcome every obs-tacle. Rather, "Our help is in the name of the Lord, who made heaven and earth."[6] In the spirit of the psalmist, Ciszek comes to his conclusion: His guilt and shame are justified, not for giving in, but for expecting that he wouldn't. In doing so, he has relied on vanity, seeing himself as his salvation and his god.

> It had been a moment of utter failure on my part to abandon myself to God's will in total Christian commitment ... But that moment of failure was in itself a great grace ... I had ... expected the Spirit to instruct me that I might conquer my interrogator, my persecutor. How foolish and how selfish! It was not the Church that was on trial in Lubianka. It was not the Soviet government or the NKGB versus Walter Ciszek. It was God versus Walter Ciszek. God was testing me in this experience, like gold in the furnace, to see how much self remained after all of my prayers and professions of faith in his will.[7]

Ciszek concludes that he had failed to recognize his total dependence on God for everything, including his life. As he later develops this insight, he learns to accept that God's will is not something hidden but manifest in the people and events presented to him in a given day. To surrender to God's will is to trust without reservation that God is in fact real and present, loving and protecting him in his providence. This act of faith evades many believers – we are always negotiating, setting conditions, cutting compromises with our plans and desires so that we can feel ourselves to be in control. But if we think, even a bit, that we are masters of our fate, to that extent we deny God's existence and refuse his presence to us in daily life.

Such an act of total surrender or abandonment is not quietism. The abandoned person does not lie around in bed, waiting for things to happen. As Ciszek puts it, each person and event presented in a given moment offers a chance to act as Christ would act, to act out of love. He acts many times in the story that follows this incident: performing liturgies in secret; counseling and helping secret Christians; acting to preserve his own life as best he can. His point is that we must surrender our illusions, our pointless strivings, our confidence in ourselves who are only as strong as our shifting circumstances permit. We must accept our weakness and our fragility.

It should be obvious that the ideal of abandonment is not restricted to priests or to Jesuits or to the victims of KGB interrogation. Ciszek's experience is dramatic in its details, but universal in its structure. How many parents of young children find their visions of domestic bliss completely shattered against the hard realities of life? They may seek control, through parenting techniques, childcare, or simple escape, throwing themselves into any work that isn't child-related. These tactics may be understandable or even wise. But in the end, for a Christian, all must be placed in God's hands, that is, under the aspect of reality. We are very weak and limited beings in fact. It is only our imagination, fed by fear, pain, mistrust, and selfishness, that leads us to think otherwise.

We may be ingenious in our attempts to hide our own helplessness from ourselves, and the richer and more privileged we are, the easier it will be. If the rubber does not hit the road in personal relationships, or at work, it comes through an accident, illness, disability, or the prospect of death.

I admit myself to be stubborn in this respect, in part thanks to the great good luck that has dogged me throughout my life. But I remind myself of the one time, lucky as I am, that I was seriously ill. I had made first promises at Madonna House and was living in the community and restoring donated antiques for the gift shop. I had spent an afternoon picking wild raspberries, up and down the wilderness. Under one raspberry plant grew a humble shoot of poison ivy. It brushed my leg; the skin reacted in a rash; the rash became seriously infected; and one day I woke up with my lower leg twice its natural size. We tried oral antibiotics, which failed. Two or three days later, I felt woozy and strange. I could not think straight. I was terrified that I had blood poisoning, or perhaps a dangerous level of allergic reaction. I panicked and called an ambulance. They put me on IV antibiotics, to be administered every eight hours, in between which I would go home. Early on at the hospital, hungry, frightened, and exhausted, I made constant demands of the nurse and burst into tears and whining when they were not immediately met. My behavior was so offensive that she complained to a member of the community. I had been reduced to the moral and intellectual capacities of a two-year-old. I was not a trained scholar in classical philosophy. I was not an upbeat, charming high achiever. I was not funny, kind, considerate, or wise. I was a mere frightened animal without a character, laid low by a piece of vegetable matter.

The greatest obstacle between God and us, in the insight of Walter Ciszek, is our belief in ourselves. The spiritual value of abandonment can in this way be seen as a willing acceptance of the mercy of God. Even one's sinfulness and selfishness must be accepted, not as immediately subject to one's will, and so to correction, but as fuel for the love of God.[8] As Paul describes his struggle to be freed of a weakness:

> Three times I begged the Lord about this, that it might leave me, but he said to me, "My grace is sufficient for you, for power is made perfect in weakness." I will rather boast most gladly of my weaknesses, in order that the power of Christ may dwell with me. Therefore, I am content with weaknesses, insults, hardships, persecutions, and constraints, for the sake of Christ; for when I am weak, then I am strong.[9]

Abandonment is in this way a needed corrective to a moralized Christianity, where one might think, from listening to Christians, that right living is the final end. To live rightly is not available by a simple exercise of the will. It requires humility, and thanks to the fragility and weakness of the human moral capacities, grounds for humility are never lacking.

Walter Ciszek does not say it, but abandonment is freedom. It is a freedom of a scope and depth that is truly terrifying to behold, because it involves accepting, as from the loving hand of God, the worst things that can possibly happen to a person, humanly speaking. (I say, humanly speaking, because to a Christian, the loss of God is the worst thing.) I mentioned earlier the true story of the Trappist monks in Algeria in the 1990s who discerned to stay in their monastery in the face of imminent murderous violence. In the film version of their story, the monks make this discernment, one by one, over the course of two weeks. The abbot visits each monk for a frank conversation. As I related, it is at this point that the abbot encourages a younger monk, in a panic over the decision: "You have already given up your life!" The abbot also speaks to the monk who serves as the local doctor. The doctor shrugs his shoulders at his impending death, telling the abbot, "I am a free man."

I am persuaded that without embracing Christian freedom as an ideal mode of life, we do not have a conception of the human good or human flourishing or human freedom that is truly available to everyone. We may imagine that secular liberal freedom – the freedom to choose one's social roles; or secular illiberal freedom – membership in a caring community – is *in principle* available to everyone, and so one may be fiercely motivated to participate in vast movements to spread it abroad. But we might consider, the merits of those merely human freedoms aside, whether we truly believe that the universal claim to human flourishing rests on our political machinations. Is it not far more attractive, more deeply egalitarian, to find a notion of freedom that can be practiced anywhere, in all circumstances, by absolutely any human being? Would not such a belief be necessary, if we are ever to be reconciled to the world as it is, shredded as it always has been and always will be by natural disaster, murderous violence, war, exploitation, and the predation of the rich on the poor?

Human weakness is one thing; death and annihilation, something different. The fear of the first is overcome more easily than the fear of the others. I will tell two more stories, each from the Second World War, perhaps because I am old enough that this period of time, endured by my grandparents, has shaped so much of the way I see the world.

Facing Death

What freedom do we express when, like the Trappists of Algeria, we choose to allow ourselves to be murdered? How might it be seen as the greatest of freedoms? Consider the life of Edith Stein, canonized under her religious name as St. Teresa Benedicta of the Cross.

Edith Stein was born in 1891 into a large Jewish family in Breslau, Germany, on Yom Kippur, the Day of Atonement.[10] Her father died when she was young, leaving her mother in charge of a large lumber business. Edith's mother became a powerful woman in the local community. She treasured her Jewish faith and passed on to her children her own awe at moral excellence and her abhorrence of sin.

Edith herself was an atheist from a young age but took an intense interest in philosophy. It did not take long for her brilliance to be recognized by her professor – at that time the most famous philosopher in Europe – Edmund Husserl. Edith threw herself joyously into the intellectual life of Husserl's circle, seeking insight with her friends into the nature of knowledge and the puzzle of its grounding in human experience.

A handful of her circle had undergone conversions to Catholicism, and Stein was curious. Her conversion came on the day when she picked up and read the Life of St. Teresa of Avila in one sitting. She finished the book, set it down, and said, "That is the truth." She was baptized as a

Catholic in 1922, beginning a painful fracture with her grief-stricken Jewish mother.

We are accustomed to a world in which women run large businesses or get doctorates in philosophy at major universities. We expect, too, that those of different religions will mix in the world of work and study, and that one might set down one religion and pick up another without serious consequences. Still, even fifty years before Edith took up her studies, it would have been unthinkable for a woman – and difficult for a Jew – to study philosophy at a German university.

Edith Stein's early life, her career and her conversion, was shaped by the freedom of movement that characterizes contemporary liberalism. So was her rejection of the faith of her parents. Edith chose her social roles, rather than accepting them as given, exemplifying a type of freedom familiar to our secular liberal frame of mind. She found the familiar limitations to this type of freedom: residual prejudice. She was Husserl's favorite student, but thanks to her gender and her ethnicity, she could not find stable work teaching philosophy in a university. The deep-rooted anti-Semitism of the Europe of earlier centuries, which had retreated enough to allow German Jews to assimilate almost completely into common life, was beginning to re-emerge.

The liberal freedom Edith received from her environment and used so fearlessly was not enough for her. She sought a greater freedom, the Christian freedom of total renunciation. Shortly after her conversion, she felt a call to be a Carmelite nun. Her spiritual director discouraged her. By this time, Edith was in demand as a Catholic speaker and writer. She taught young women at an excellent Catholic school until finding a post as a lecturer in Münster. Her advisors thought she was doing more good in the world than she could ever do from a monastery.

At this point comes the moment of Edith's greatest freedom, a freedom before which we should stand utterly astonished. Adolf Hitler is elected chancellor of Germany in 1933. Shortly thereafter, he issues an edict forbidding any Jew to work at a German university. Husserl's favorite student, a popular speaker and writer, a devoted and beloved teacher, was out of work.

Edith understood, as few in her moment did, exactly what Hitler intended for the Jews. She wrote an impassioned letter to the Pope, expressing her grave concern at the moral and spiritual cost of Catholic complicity with the Nazi government. She knew that real violence lurked behind the civil and legal restrictions.

When Edith lost her job, then, she met with a sudden total rejection from her community, along with the prospect of exile or violent death. It is hard to imagine a worse moment for anyone. Yet for her, it was a moment of joy. "Could it be time to go to Carmel?" she wondered.

Her call to the convent was not, as it might seem, an escape into hiding and its safety. She understood that her vocation was to offer her life as a sacrifice, with and for the Jewish people. And so it was.

She entered the Carmel at Breslau within a few months of Hitler's edict. She confined herself to a cloister, her only contact with friends and family reduced to occasional conversations through a grille. The distinguished philosophy professor mopped floors and sewed habits with her sisters in the monastery. While her superiors asked her to keep writing books and essays, few in the cloister had any idea of who she was. To them, Sister Teresa Benedicta was a fervent and joyful older woman, perhaps a bit less competent at practical tasks than the others.

The broader dimension of her vocation unfolded alongside its more typical milestones. Within ten days of Edith's profession of final vows in April 1938, Nazi officials came to the convent, to ensure that all the nuns voted in an election affirming Hitler. Edith did not believe in practical accommodation to evil, even when common sense demanded it. She had urged the nuns to vote no. Before she could vote no herself, the officials discovered that she was of "non-Aryan" descent. Edith knew she had to leave the convent, and quickly, for her own safety and for that of the other nuns. She was transferred to another Carmel in the Netherlands, at that time safe from Nazi interference.

The relative safety lasted only a few years. In July 1942, the occupying Nazis took measures to round up the Jewish people living in the Netherlands, agreeing to spare Christian converts. Dissatisfied with the concession, the Dutch Catholic bishops wrote a letter of protest and ordered it read in all the parishes. The letter stands today as a rare and eloquent public expression of resistance to the Nazi genocide. It was the sort of honest moral confrontation that Edith had implored from the Pope years earlier.

The Nazis, as the cliché goes, left no good deed unpunished. They took vengeance on the defiant bishops by rounding up 300 Catholics of Jewish descent, including Catholic religious, and shipping them to the gas chambers at Auschwitz.

On August 2, 1942, a knock came at the door of the convent during Vespers. It was the SS, seeking Edith, along with her sister and fellow convert Rosa who lived there. The Stein sisters had sought transit papers to Switzerland. The papers had been approved but had not arrived in time. It was reported but not verified that Edith spoke to her sister as they left the monastery: "Come, we go for our people."

The Stein sisters disappeared into the column of victims traveling east. Survivors later reported a serene woman in a Carmelite habit, comforting and aiding others as she could, all the way to her death and immolation. It was the death that Edith had foreseen and chosen. The smoke of her burned body, rising from the crematorium, was for her an offering of incense, in gratitude for her ultimate union with her Lord and Savior.

Stein knew and lived out the teaching of abandonment as Paul wrote in his famous hymn in the Letter to the Romans:

> What will separate us from the love of Christ? Will anguish, or distress, or persecution, or famine, or nakedness, or peril, or the sword? As it is written:
> "For your sake we are being slain all the day;
> we are looked upon as sheep to be slaughtered."
> No, in all these things we conquer overwhelmingly through him who loved us.
> For I am convinced that neither death, nor life, nor angels, nor principalities, nor present things, nor future things, nor powers, nor height, nor depth, nor any other creature will be able to separate us from the love of God in Christ Jesus our Lord.[11]

Facing Annihilation

Is there anything worse than death? As I suggested in the first chapter, it is worse for us to think or to believe that our future will be annihilated, that we are in the last generation of human beings, or even just to see the projects in which we have concretely placed our future turned to dust.[12] We can rely on science fiction scenarios, such as *Children of Men*; we can read the direst predictions of climate scientists. But I wonder if we can also look at the experiences of those who went through something close to annihilation, the atom bomb.

The nuclear scientist and doctor Takashi Nagai was working at his research hospital in Nagasaki on August 9, 1945.[13] He was dean of radiology, a Catholic convert, a husband, and father of two young children. He and a handful of colleagues happened to be working in concrete buildings when the atom bomb hit. The concrete saved their lives, but their lives were dramatically changed in an instant. Nagai reports the experience of a professor of pharmacology who had been digging a shelter with his students when the bomb hit and survived because he was underground at the time. He emerged from the tunnel and looked around in shock:

> The large buildings of the Department of Pharmacy were no longer there. The pharmacology classroom was not there. The fence was not there. The houses outside the fence were not there. Everything had disappeared, and all that remained was a sea of fire.[14]

His students whom he had been working with lay dead around him. Whole university buildings had disappeared:

the tiled houses of the residential districts, the factories. Great trees lay pulled up by their roots. Every scrap of vegetation had died. The burned and mutilated bodies of the dying and dead lay everywhere.

Nagai's own children were spared, but his wife and home had evaporated. His memoir is astonishing in its capacity to take in the human cost without losing the objectivity of the nuclear scientist. He looks at his surroundings, learning from what he sees, on the basis of what he already knows. He and his colleagues turn immediately to caring for the wounded. They eat a meal of pumpkins, cooked on a fire in metal helmets. They build makeshift shelters and work tirelessly for one another. They are told that the war is over: Emperor Hirohito has surrendered. They are despondent: Everything they have worked for, large and small, has turned to dust. The war effort has been for nothing. The operating room, carefully designed for a response to a bombing, has been destroyed, the disaster-response training irrelevant. Even in the broader picture: Ten years of specimens, all the records of their research, all are burned to ash.

Nagai did not flee the scene to rebuild a normal life. On the contrary, he built a simple hut near the ruins of the university, in order to remember and to contemplate the bombing and its meaning. He stayed there, with his children and his mother-in-law, for the rest of his life. The great insight came a few months later, when he was asked to speak at a funeral service in the ruins of the cathedral for the dead.

As Nagai saw it, the connection between the bombing of Nagasaki and the emperor's surrender were mysterious. At the same time as the bombing, the Supreme Council of War was meeting to discuss their response to the bombing of Hiroshima. The council was split; the meeting, inconclusive; either way, the emperor's role was only ceremonial. The emperor called the council together again at midnight, in a breach of protocol. Emperor Hirohito made known his decision to surrender, another breach of custom and protocol. At the same time, the cathedral in Nagasaki exploded. As Nagai saw it, Nagasaki had been offered as a sacrifice in atonement for all the crimes of the Second World War.

Nagasaki was the Catholic center of Japan; the faith had been practiced since the Jesuit missionaries of the seventeenth century and their converts underwent persecutions of overwhelming cruelty. As far as Nagai was concerned, it was the prayers and the suffering of the dead faithful that ended the war. Nagai's prayer was that the sacrifice would suffice that an atomic weapon would never fall on the earth again.

In an address at a large funeral service for the victims of the bombings, Nagai said:

> The human family has inherited the sin of Adam who ate the fruit of the forbidden tree; we have inherited the sin of Cain who killed his younger brother; we have forgotten we are children of God; we have believed in idols; we have disobeyed the law of love. Joyfully we have hated one another, joyfully we have killed one another. And now at last we have brought this great and evil war to an end.

Then, Nagai makes the great act of abandonment:

> How noble, how splendid was that holocaust of August 9, when flames soared from the cathedral, dispelling the darkness of war and bringing the light of peace!

and echoes the words of Job:

> The Lord has given, the Lord has taken away. Blessed be
> the name of the Lord!

Nagai's speech met with anger from the listeners, on the charge that he was justifying the murder of their loved ones. His memoir, which laid out the effects of the bomb in cold detail and ended with his speech at the funeral, could not be published for several years. The occupying general, Douglas MacArthur, would only let it past the censors if it were published with an account of Japanese war crimes in the Pacific. Nagai continued to write and to speak on behalf of peace and disarmament. Like the murdered Trappist doctor in Algeria, he was a free man.

It is easy to be offended by Nagai's embrace of the bombing of Nagasaki as an instrument of grace, as his contemporaries were. Yet those of us who are theists must be serious. How is the atom bomb different in principle from the smaller-scale evils we know that God permits on a regular basis? When does the divine will relax either its power or its benevolence so that we are not called to seek our good in it and to love God and our neighbor more rather than less?

To speak as Nagai does is not to deny the reality or the validity of grief, or to whitewash real evil. It is to see all of these things and take them to heart in light of a benevolent, all-loving, all-powerful God. Theologians are fond of the distinction between God's "permissive" will and his "active will," and of saying that God never actively wills evil. Yet willed permission is still an exercise of will, and one must ask how that permission is meant as an act of love for us personally. Otherwise, Christian life will only ever be lukewarm, a pious hobby lived in relative luxury, where one thanks oneself under the guise of thanking God. Only with the practice of abandonment and its freedom can Christianity fulfill its promise of consolation in the face of the worst suffering or its deepest, most luminous and sparkling promise, the promise of happiness.

Conclusion
The Last Things

I began with an account of the contingency of human achievement and the futility of human endeavor. I have argued that our contemporary theorists of the meaning of life have failed us. They have failed us for the simple reason that they, like all of us, hide from the contingency and the fragility of things. Nothing keeps our cities from becoming Nagasaki. Nothing keeps our careers from being dashed like Edith Stein's. Nothing keeps the whole sphere of our endeavor, work, love, family, all of it, from complete oblivion, from being erased in a heartbeat. Indeed, one way or another, it will all be erased. One day, nothing will be left of anything we care about.

True, we cannot always keep this reality in mind. We would lose our minds if we did. I have not made an argument for Christianity. I am skeptical of such arguments. The use of reason, in my view, is critical. It can show up falsehood and inconsistency, as Augustine discovered in his search for wisdom through philosophy, but its capacity to break through the motivated rationalizations that keep us from reality is limited. That is not to deny the power in our multiple tools for understanding, the objects of everyday experience, of nature and human community, thousands of years of books, brimming with wisdom, in multiple traditions. We have ways of life, handed down from generation to generation, which point to realities that cannot always be grasped in an instant or justified in clear and simple principles. They require reflection, in a spirit of openness and driven by hunger for a solution to the basic catastrophe of human existence.

Faith is a gift of grace, not effort; it is not under our control. I have no illusions about my own capacity to transmit it. Nor have I achieved the state of abandonment or surrender which I report. On the contrary, I nurse my grievances and contrive my success much like everyone else. Faith does not sink into one's soul all in an instant. There is a simple basis, given in baptism and nurtured by basic teaching, but it must be left to bear fruit in its own time and in its own ways.

I have left out something that would be very surprising to all of the renunciants I have discussed: eternal life. It is a glaring omission. Surrender is possible, I suspect, only in the depth of faith required to see with clarity that death is not the end of human life but a beginning of a different kind of life. Such a life is not the everlasting pursuit of the same old thing, as philosophers, building straw men, have charged. As Paul says, "we shall be changed."[1] We know eternal life in the same way that St. John of the Cross suggested we knew God. For John of the Cross, we know God in mortal life only in intense spiritual darkness: through pain, and as the pain points to, the ferocity of our longing for him.

I am afraid I have suggested that pain and darkness are the ultimate reality about human flourishing. But that is true only in mortal life. In the realm of eternal life, pain, darkness, and suffering will be lifted away so that the full promise of human happiness may be fulfilled. We know this, as Julian of Norwich and Takashi Nagai knew it, even before we die. We know it through our capacity to accept all things as good, all the people and circumstances of daily life, all as from the hand of a loving God.

We often imagine that faith is dying in North America and Europe because of our scientific and intellectual sophistication. I think there is a simpler explanation, one that I have suggested in these pages. It is our enormous wealth that destroys our faith. It is comfort and security that permits us to delude ourselves that we are pure consciousness, free of the humble meat that constitutes us; that we have control over our destinies and our moral condition; that death can be evaded with the pleasures of work and family, even that the future promised by children is unnecessary to make sense of our daily activities.

None of the preceding thoughts about life and its meaning are my own bright ideas. It is the longtime testimony of ancient wisdom, communicated in the Hebrew Bible and lived out by generations of courageous men and women who renounced everything – wealth, first and foremost – for a true love that offered to transform their lives and the lives of every human being. I am hardly adequate in learning or in action to bear such a message. I hope that this little book has encouraged you, intrigued you, even infuriated you to investigate it yourself.

NOTES

What Is This Book About?

1 Matthew 19:16–24; Mark 10:17–22.
2 Athanasius of Alexandria, *The Life of Antony*, trans. T. Vivian and A. N. Athanassakis (Kalamazoo, MI: Cistercian Publications, 2003).
3 Sulpicius Severus, *On The Life of Saint Martin*, trans. A. Roberts, in *Nicene and Post-Nicene Fathers*, Second Series, vol. 11, rev. and ed. K. Knight (www.newadvent.org/fathers/3501 .htm), chapters 3 and 4.
4 Bonaventure, *The Life of Saint Francis of Assisi*, trans. B. Fahey; chapters 1 and 2, in *St Francis of Assisi: Writings and Early Biographies*, ed. M. Habig (Chicago, IL: Franciscan Herald Press, 1973), pp. 635–646.
5 1 Kings 19:9–12.
6 2 Kings 1:7–8.
7 John Cassian, *The Institutes*, I.1, 11, trans. Boniface Ramsey (New York: Newman Press, 2000).
8 *Epistle to Diognetus*, chapters 5 and 6, in Cyril C. Richardson, *Early Christian Fathers* (Philadelphia, PA: The Westminster Press, 1953).
9 1 Corinthians 15:31.
10 "The Life of Saint Mary of Egypt," in *The Great Canon of St Andrew of Crete and The Life of Saint Mary of Egypt*, trans. Abbess Thekla and Mother Katherine, ed. Fr Christopher Wallace (n.p.: Finnan Books, 2013), pp. 106–138.
11 My account of abandonment here and in what follows is very much influenced by Jean-Pierre Caussade, *Abandonment to*

163

Divine Providence, trans. John Beevers (New York: Image, 1975).

12 1 Corinthians 13:12.

13 1 Corinthians 9:19–23.

14 See Dismas de Lasus, *Risques et dérives de la vie religieuse* (Paris: Editions de Cerf, 2020).

Introduction

1 Daniel Fanous, *A Silent Patriarch: Kyrillos VI (1902–1971) Life and Legacy* (Yonkers, NY: St. Vladimir's Seminary Press, 2019), 67.

2 Romans 6:4.

3 1 Corinthians 15:31.

4 *Republic* 548a; Aristotle, *Politics* 1269b20 ff., 1270a11 ff.

5 Revelation 3:16–17.

6 Genesis 3.

7 Aristotle, *Nicomachean Ethics* 10.7, 1177b31–1178a2; Ross translation.

8 See my "Degenerate Regimes in Plato's Republic," in M. McPherran, ed. *The Cambridge Critical Guide to Plato's Republic* (Cambridge: Cambridge University Press, 2010).

9 Philippians 2:6–8.

10 Philippians 2:9–10.

11 John 21:15–19.

Chapter 1

1 Galawdewos, *The Life and Struggles of Our Mother Walatta Petros*, trans. W. Belcher and M. Kleiner (Princeton, NJ: Princeton University Press, 2015), pp. 93–97.

2 *Ibid.*, p. 97.

3 Alternately, Galawdewos calls it "the filthy faith of Leo" (*Ibid.*, pp. 122, 155). The Ethiopian church had rejected the Council of Chalcedon (451 CE), presided over by Leo the Great, and followed the patriarch of Alexandria, Dioscorus, instead. Leo held Christ to have two natures, one divine, one human; Dioscorus emphasized the unity from the two natures.

4 *Ibid.*, p. 200.

5 Quoted in Sergei Hackel, *Pearl of Great Price: The Life of Mother Maria Skobtsova 1891–1945* (Crestwood, NY: St. Vladimir's Seminary Press, 1981), pp. 5–6.

6 Teresa of Avila, *Foundations*, in *The Complete Works of St Teresa of Jesus*, vol. 2, trans. E. Allison Peers (London and New York: Sheed and Ward, 1946), p. 52.

7 Teresa of Avila, *Foundations*, p. 56.

8 Willa Cather, *Death Comes for the Archbishop* (New York: Knopf, 1927).

9 Guillaume de Tocco, *L'histoire de saint Thomas d'Aquin*, trans. Claire Le Brun-Gouanvic (Paris: Éditions du Cerf, 2005); chapters 1–12.

10 Not only *The Sound of Music*, but also the famous nun movies *Bells of St. Marys* (1945) and *The Trouble with Angels* (1966) contain this claim.

11 Ecclesiastes 1:4, 9.

12 Ecclesiastes 2:14.

13 I owe this insight to Fr. Denis Lemieux.

14 Ecclesiastes 5:14; cf. Job 1:21.

15 Job 21:7; cf. Ecclesiastes 7:15.

16 Ecclesiastes 9:2, 3; cf. Job 9:22.

17 Ecclesiastes 3:14; Job 9:19.

18 Ecclesiastes 11:5; Job 9:10.

19 Ecclesiastes 2:17, 4:2; Job 3:3 ff.

20 Thomas Nagel, "The Absurd," *Journal of Philosophy* 68:20 (1971), 716–727.

21 See Samuel Scheffler, *Death and the Afterlife* (Oxford: Oxford University Press, 2014), p. 22.

22 As is suggested by Seana Shiffrin, "Preserving the Valued or Preserving Valuing?" in *ibid.*, pp. 147–149.

23 This is why, I think, Kieran Setiya's attempt to ground the meaning of life in "atelic" experiences, experiences complete in themselves, is a failure. He is quite right to distinguish the value of such experiences from the value of finite achievements. But atelic experiences depend on objects, which in turn are susceptible to annihilation. See Setiya, "The Mid-Life Crisis," *Philosopher's Imprint* 14:31 (2014) and *Midlife: A Philosophical Guide* (Princeton, NJ: Princeton University Press, 2019), chapter 6.

24 Eleanore Stump, *Wandering in Darkness* (Oxford: Oxford University Press, 2010).

25 As argued by Scheffler, *Death and the Afterlife*, and Bernard Williams, "The Makropoulos Case: Reflections on the Tedium of Immortality," in *Problems of the Self* (Cambridge: Cambridge University Press, 1973), pp. 82–100.

26 Also discussed (in its novel form) by Scheffler, *Death and the Afterlife*, and Setiya, *Life Is Hard* (New York: Penguin, 2022).

27 Sam Scheffler in *Death and the Afterlife* notices that the future of humanity lies in the background of our thinking. If the prospect of that future is removed, meaning disappears. But I think he is too sanguine about meaning in the face of certain destruction after an indefinite time. He considers our continued pursuit of our various projects as a sign that such destruction does not undermine their meaning. I think it is more plausible that we simply cannot face the meaninglessness of most of our activity.

28 Scheffler rejects this concern, on the grounds, it seems, that distant prospects of annihilation do not trouble us (Scheffler, *Death and the Afterlife*, pp. 62–64). In his response to his critics, he considers the possibility that our behavior may be

incoherent (as I think it is) (*ibid.*, pp. 188–190). Setiya develops the difficulty in the ways I have suggested but argues that certain activities will still matter in the last generation. I think the gulf between our pursuits when we ignore the end of the world and when we are imminently aware of it cannot be bridged so easily. (Setiya, *Life Is Hard*, chapter 6).

29 Ecclesiastes 3:11.
30 Ecclesiastes 8:5–6.
31 Ecclesiastes 3:11. In Hebrew, the word *ha olam* can be translated either as "the world" or as "the forever," the timeless or eternal.
32 Ecclesiastes 1:8.
33 See the brilliant discussion of chronic pain in Setiya, *Life Is Hard*.
34 Homer, *Iliad* 16.772.
35 In Helga Kuhse and Peter Singer (eds.), *Bioethics: An Anthology* (Oxford: Blackwell, 2006), pp. 266–275.
36 Quoted in Hackel, *Pearl of Great Price*, p. 4.
37 Augustine, *Confessions* I.1.

Chapter 2

1 Hackel, *Pearl of Great Price*, p. 6.
2 I discuss this in somewhat more detail in the preface to my *Lost in Thought: The Hidden Pleasures of an Intellectual Life* (Princeton, NJ: Princeton University Press, 2020).
3 Pierre Raphael, *Inside Rikers Island: A Chaplain's Search for God* (Maryknoll, NY: Orbis, 1990), p. 28.
4 "Life of St. Pelagia the Harlot," in Benedicta Ward, *Harlots of the Desert* (Trappist, KY: Cistercian Publications, 1987); "Pelagia of Antioch" in *Holy Women of the Syrian Orient*, trans. S. Brock and S. Harvey (Berkeley and London: University of California Press, 1998); "Saint Marina, Virgin," in Jacobus de

Voraigne, *The Golden Legend: Readings on the Saints*, vol. 1, trans. William Granger Ryan (Princeton, NJ: Princeton University Press, 1993), pp. 324–325.

5 Matthew 5:3–10.

6 Psalm 9:13; cf. Psalm 72:4; Psalm 132:15; Proverbs 21:13.

7 Theodoret of Cyrrhus, *A History of the Monks of Syria*, trans. R. M. Price (Kalamazoo, MI: Cistercian Publications, 1985), pp. 160–161.

8 *Ibid.*, p. 165. Forty-eight years adds the twenty-eight years his contemporary Theodoret reports to the twenty years that passed in between Theodoret's writing and Simeon's death in 459.

9 Psalm 1, my translation.

10 Psalm 37:35–36 (Psalm 36 in editions following the Vulgate), trans. the Grail; *The Grail Psalms: A New Translation* (London: Collins, 1963).

11 Psalm 73:28.

12 As Psalm 139 describes.

13 Søren Kierkegaard, *Philosophical Fragments*, IV.195–IV.201, trans. H. V. Hong and E. H. Hong (Princeton, NJ: Princeton University Press, 1985), pp. 26–34; quotation from pp. 32–33.

14 Kim Phuc Phan Thi, *Fire Road: The Napalm Girl's Journey through the Horrors of War to Faith, Forgiveness, and Peace* (n. p.: Tyndale Momentum, 2017), pp. 97–99.

15 My source for the life of Bakhita, unless marked otherwise, is Roberto Zanini, *Bakhita: From Slave to Saint* (San Francisco, CA: Ignatius, 2013).

16 Cf. Zanini, *Bakhita: From Slave to Saint*, p. 190.

17 Quoted in *ibid.*, p. 79. Bakhita's short autobiography is also printed in its entirety in Maria Luisa Dagnino, *Bakhita Tells Her Story*, 3rd ed. (Rome: Casa Generalizia, Canossiane Figlie della Carità, 1993).

18 Zanini, *Bakhita: From Slave to Saint*, p. 89.

19 Dagnino, *Bakhita Tells Her Story*, p. 109.

20 *Ibid.*, p. 103.

21 For an account of the lives of Bakhita, Margaret, and others as survivors of sexual abuse, see Dawn Eden Goldstein, *My Peace I Give You: Healing Sexual Wounds with the Help of the Saints* (Notre Dame, IN: Ave Maria Press, 2012).

22 Fr. William Bonniwell, OP, *The Life of Blessed Margaret of Castello* (Rockford, IL: TAN, 1983).

23 "The Life of Saint Mary of Egypt." Cf. also Ward, *Harlots of the Desert*.

24 "Pelagia of Antioch," in *Holy Women of the Syrian Orient*.

25 See the Great Canon of St. Andrew of Crete 2.3, discussed in Olivier Clement, *The Song of Tears*, trans. Michael Donley (Yonkers, NY: St. Vladimir's Press, 2021), chapter 4. See also 1 Timothy 15.

26 James Baldwin, "Why I Stopped Hating Shakespeare," in *The Cross of Redemption: Uncollected Writings*, ed. Randall Kenan (New York: Vintage Random House, 2010), pp. 65–69.

27 Luke 6:20–26.

28 So I take to be the suggestion of his warning against the "military-industrial complex" in his farewell address as president on January 17, 1961 (https://avalon.law.yale.edu/20th_century/eisenhower001.asp).

29 Cf. for instance, Siddharth Kara, "Is Your Phone Tainted by the Misery of 35,000 Children in Congo's Mines?," *The Guardian*, October 12, 2018, https://bit.ly/3ak5l3A; Henry Sanderson, "Congo, Child Labour, and Your Car," *Financial Times*, July 7, 2019, www.ft.com/content/c6909812-9ce4-11e9-9c06-a4640c9feebb; Nicholas Niarkos, "The Dark Side of Congo's Cobalt Rush," *New Yorker*, May 24, 2021, https://bit.ly/3PbYmsg.

30 Phil Jones, *Work without the Worker: Labour in the Age of Platform Capitalism* (London and New York: Verso, 2021).

31 My sources for Catherine's life are her autobiography, Catherine de Hueck Doherty, *Fragments of My Life* (Notre

Dame, IN: Ave Maria Press, 1979); and Lorene Duquin, *They Called Her the Baroness* (New York: Alba House, 1995).

32 Duquin, *They Called Her the Baroness*, pp. 50–51.

33 Since this book may be read by philosophers, I cannot resist relating that Catherine, while working for the lecture bureau, met Bertrand Russell, who insisted that she sleep with him. She refused him, saying, "Have you looked in the mirror lately?" *Ibid.*, p. 109.

34 As for instance in Doherty, *Poustinia* (Combermere, ON: Madonna House Books, 2000).

Chapter 3

1 Fanous, *A Silent Patriarch*, pp. 134–135.

2 1 Corinthians 13:3

3 Fr. Walter Ciszek, SJ, *He Leadeth Me* (Garden City, NY: Doubleday, 1973), pp. 51–52.

4 Charles Peguy, *Basic Verities*, trans. Anne and Julian Green (New York: Pantheon Books, 1943), pp. 206–207.

5 See Sr. Dolores Hart, OSB, with Richard De Neut, *The Ear of the Heart: An Actress's Journey from Hollywood to Holy Vows* (San Francisco, CA: Ignatius Press, 2013).

6 See Peter Brown, *Augustine of Hippo: A Biography* (Berkeley: University of California Press, 2013).

7 "The Life of St. Odo," cited in C. H. Lawrence, *Medieval Monasticism*, 2nd ed. (London and New York: Longman, 1989), p.89.

8 As instructed in the Rule of St. Benedict; *The Rule of St. Benedict*, trans. L. Dysinger (Santa Ana, CA: Source Books, 1997), chapter 42.

9 See, for example, on Psalm 139: Hilary of Poitiers *Tractatus super Psalmos* (Turnholti: Brepols, 1997); Augustine,

Expositions of the Psalms 121–150, trans. Maria Boulding (New York: New City Press), pp. 256–282; Cassiodorus, *Explanation of the Psalms*, trans. P. G. Walsh, vol. 3 (New York and Mahweh, NJ: Paulist Press).

10 Augustine, *Confessions*, trans. F. Sheed (New York: Sheed and Ward, 1943), 8.12.30.

11 Hebrews 4:12–13.

12 Raymond of Capua, *The Life of St. Catherine of Siena*, trans. George Lamb (Rockford, IL: Tan Books, 2003), 146–149.

13 Genesis 28:10–19.

14 Genesis 32:14–33.

15 Mark 1:12–13; Matthew 4:1–11; Luke 4:1–13.

16 See discussion in Ron Haflidson, *On Solitude, Conscience, Love, and Our Inner and Outer Lives* (London and New York: Bloomsbury T & T Clark, 2019), pp. 33–41.

17 Matthew 6:5–6.

18 I am indebted to Ron Haflidson for pointing to the interest of this term, although I do not think it means "storeroom" in the New Testament, as I explain here. Augustine's use ["the bedroom is the heart"], even if it relies on a Latin translation (*cubiculum*) is closer to the original sense (Haflidson, *On Solitude*; 41, 41n, 56).

19 As for instance in Aesop, Fable 15, line 5; Thucydides 7.24.2; Plato, *Republic* 416d7, 548a7, 550d7.

20 The comic poet Menander refers to a temperate woman as a "*tamieion* of virtue" (Frag 1109.1). Plutarch calls the memory a "storehouse [*tamieion*] of learning" (*Moralia*, "The Education of Children," 9D); and, citing Democritus, speaks of the human interior as "an intricate and tumultuous storehouse [*tamieion*] and treasury of evils" (*Moralia*, "Whether the Affections of the Soul are Worse Than Those of the Body," 500E).

21 Septuagint (LXX) Genesis 43:30.

22 LXX Exodus 7:28.

23 LXX Judges 16:9, 12.

24 LXX Judges 3:24.

25 LXX 2 Samuel 13:10; 1 Kings 15.

26 LXX 1 Kings 21:30, 22:25.

27 LXX 2 Kings 9:1–6.

28 LXX 2 Kings 6:12.

29 Luke 12:2–3.

30 LXX Song of Songs 1:4, 3:4, 8:2.

31 Tobit 7:15–18.

32 LXX Proverbs 20:27.

33 Augustine, *Expositions on the Psalms*, 35.5; cited in Haflidson, *On Solitude*, p. 56.

34 LXX Psalms of Solomon 14:8.

35 *Summa Theologiae* II.II Q83 A1.

36 Quoted in James M. Lang, "Love Means Answering the Mail," *Commonweal*, November 27, 2021, www .commonwealmagazine.org/love-means-answering-mail.

37 Herbert McCabe, OP, "Prayer," in *God Matters* (London: Chapman, 1987), p. 223.

38 Ezekiel 11:19, 36:26; Jeremiah 24:7.

39 See William O'Grady, "The Bible and the Human Heart," *St. John's Review*, 37:1 (1986), 66.

40 John of the Cross, *Dark Night of the Soul*, 1.12, in *Collected Works of St. John of the Cross*, trans. K. Kavanaugh and O. Rodriguez (Washington, DC: Institute for Carmelite Studies Publications, 2017), p. 385.

41 John of the Cross, *Dark Night of the Soul*, 1.5.2.

42 *Ibid.*, 1.6.

43 *Ibid.*, 1.3.

44 *Ibid.*, 1.7.1.

45 *Ibid.*, 1.2.1–5.

46 Graham Greene, *The Heart of the Matter* (New York: Penguin, 1971).

47 Sigrid Undset, *The Master of Hestviken*, trans. Arthur Chater (New York: Knopf, 1952). A new translation is appearing, volume by volume, under its original title: *Olav Audunssøn*, vol. 1, *Vows*, trans. Tiina Nunnally (Minneapolis: University of Minnesota Press, 2020); vol. 2, *Providence*, trans. Tiina Nunnally (Minneapolis: University of Minnesota Press, 2021).

48 *Ancrene Wisse*, part 2, in *Anchoritic Spirituality: Ancrene Wisse and Associated Works*, trans A. Savage and N. Watson (Mahwah, NJ: Paulist Press, 1991), p. 82.

49 "Holy Maidenhood," in *ibid.*, pp. 226–227.

50 *Compedium of Theology* 2.2, https://isidore.co/aquinas/english/ Compendium.htm#B2. I owe the reference to Pater Edmund Waldstein, O.Cist.

51 *Revelations of Divine Love*, trans. Dom Roger Hudleston, OSB, 2nd ed. (London: Burns Oates, 1952), chapter 10.

52 *Ibid.*

53 Luke 7:37–38.

54 *Dark Night of the Soul*, 2.13.6.

55 Cf. Thomas Aquinas, *Summa Theologiae*, Q83 A2.

56 Julian, *Revelations of Divine Love*, chapter 43.

57 *Ibid.*, chapter 27; cf. chapters. 11, 29, 31–32.

58 So I understand *Purgatorio* xxx–xxxi; the end-point of decline is *Inferno* i.

59 Kierkegaard, *Fear and Trembling*, trans. H. V. Hong and E. H. Hong (Princeton, NJ: Princeton University Press, 1983), III.85–103, pp. 33–53.

60 *The Way of a Pilgrim*, trans. Helen Bacovcin (New York and London: Image Doubleday, 1978), p.17.

61 *Ibid.*, p. 25.

62 Etty Hillesum, *An Interrupted Life: The Diaries 1941–1943 and Letters from Westerbork*, trans. A. J. Pomerans (New York: Henry Holt, 1996), p. 305.

63 *Ibid.*, p. 274.

Chapter 4

1 Deuteronomy 6:5; Leviticus 19:18.
2 Catherine Doherty, *Poustinia: Encountering God in Silence, Solitude and Prayer* (Notre Dame, IN: Ave Maria Press, 1975), p. 148.
3 Quoted in Hackel, *Pearl of Great Price*, p. 4.
4 Caryll Houselander, *A Rocking-Horse Catholic* (New York: Sheed and Ward, 1955), pp. 72–74.
5 Revelation 7:9–11.
6 Galawdewos, *The Life and Struggles of Our Mother Walatta Petros*, pp. 208–209; I modify the translation so that "virgin" is kept consistent.
7 Alec Guinness, *Blessings in Disguise* (New York: Knopf, 1986), p. 40; the whole account of the visit is delightful.
8 *Summa Theologiae*, II.II, Q 29, A 3, trans. Fathers of English Dominican Province (Notre Dame, IN: Ave Maria Press, 1948).
9 Cf. Agnes Callard's essay on the epistemic horrors of eros: "The Eros Monster," *Harpers*, March 2022, https://bit.ly/3Ir7N4R.
10 Eugene Vodolazkin, *Laurus*, trans. L. C. Hayden (London: Oneworld, 2015).
11 Catherine Doherty, *Fragments of My Life* (Notre Dame, IN: Ave Maria Press, 1979), pp. 165–166.
12 William Faulkner, *Light in August* (New York: Random House (Vintage), 1959).
13 See Wesley Yang, "The Face of Seung-Hui Cho," *n+1* no. 6 (Winter 2008), reprinted in *The Souls of Yellow Folk* (New York and London: Norton, 2018). Yang's insight is generalized by Amia Sreenivasan, "Does Anyone Have the Right to Sex?," *London Review of Books* 40:6 (22 March 2018).
14 George Orwell, *Down and Out in Paris and London* (New York and London: Harcourt, 1933, renewed 1961), chapter 2.

15 As discussed in Benedict Groeschel, *The Courage to be Chaste* (Mahwah, NJ: Paulist Press, 1985).

16 Cassian, *Institutes* IV.9; cf. *Rule of St. Benedict*, 7.44: "The fifth step of humility is when through humble confession one does not hide from one's abbot the evil thoughts that enter one's heart, nor the evils committed in secret."

17 David Graeber, *Bullshit Jobs* (New York: Simon and Schuster, 2018).

18 Aelred of Rievaulx, *De institutione inclusarum: Two English Versions*, ed. J. Ayto and A. Barratt (London and New York: Oxford University Press, 1984), MS Bodleian 423, chapter xiii, 669, p. 16.

19 Blessed Raymond of Capua, *The Life of St. Catherine of Siena*, pp. 146–149.

20 Ignatius, *Spiritual Exercises*, paragraph 146 (Third Point); 319 (Rule Six) 350 (Fifth Note); reference points from *The Spiritual Exercises of St. Ignatius Loyola*, study edition, ed. Eric Jensen, SJ, https://orientations.jesuits.ca/SpExx%20Jensen.pdf.

21 St. Thérèse of Lisieux, *Autobiography*, trans. Ronald Knox (New York: PJ Kenedy, 1958), pp. 268–269.

22 "[Some have known . . .] A girl that knew all Dante once / live to bear children to a dunce," "Why should not old men be mad?" W. B. Yeats, *Collected Poems, 1889–1939* (open source), https://bit.ly/3zqogU9.

23 Cassian, *Institutes* book 9; Thomas Aquinas, *Summa Theologiae* II.II, question 35; Jean-Charles Nault, OSB, *The Noonday Devil: Acedia, the Unnamed Evil of Our Times* (San Francisco, CA: Ignatius, 2013).

24 Luke 6:27–28.

25 Both cases are discussed in: Timothy Keller, "The Fading of Forgiveness," *Comment* May 2021, https://comment.org/the-fading-of-forgiveness/; Matt Schiavenza, "Hatred and

Forgiveness in Charleston," *The Atlantic* (June 20, 2015), https://bit.ly/3uzO7WL.

26 Cited in Dagnino, *Bakhita Tells Her Story*, p. 113.

27 Thi, *Fire Road*, p. 257

28 G. K. Chesterton, *St. Francis of Assisi* (London: Hodder and Stoughton, 1924).

29 Jacobus de Voraigne, *The Golden Legend*, section 117: The Life of St. Laurence
(Princeton: Princeton University Press, 1993) pp. 63–74. The *Legend* has Lawrence executed by Decius, but the year 258 suggests Valerian; the *Legend* author goes to great lengths to explain the discrepancy.

30 Leo I, Sermon 85, trans. Charles Lett Feltoe. From *Nicene and Post-Nicene Fathers*, Second Series, vol. 12, ed. Philip Schaff and Henry Wace (Buffalo, NY: Christian Literature Publishing Co., 1895.) Revised for New Advent by Kevin Knight, www.newadvent.org/fathers/360385.htm.

31 As reported in Paul Glynn, *A Song for Nagasaki* (San Francisco, CA: Ignatius Press, 1988), p. 186.

Chapter 5

1 My account of abandonment is very much influenced by Jean-Pierre Caussade, *Abandonment to Divine Providence*.

2 "The Leaden Echo and the Golden Echo," *The Poems of Gerard Manley Hopkins*, ed. W. H. Gardner and N. H. MacKenzie, 4th ed. (Oxford: Oxford University Press, 1970).

3 My sources are Walter Ciszek, SJ, with Daniel Flaherty, SJ, *With God in Russia* (San Francisco, CA: HarperOne, 2017); and Ciszek, *He Leadeth Me*.

4 Ciszek, *With God in Russia*, p. 8.

5 Psalm 146:3

6 Psalm 33:17; Psalm 124:8; this translation and two previous by the Grail: *The Grail Psalms: A New Translation* (London: Collins, 1963).

7 Ciszek, *He Leadeth Me*, pp. 70–71.

8 See Thérèse of Lisieux's reflection on the love of God as a furnace for sin:

"Ever since I have been given the grace to understand also the love of the Heart of Jesus, I admit that it has expelled all fear from my heart. The remembrance of my faults humbles me, draws me never to depend on my strength which is only weakness, but this remembrance speaks to love and mercy even more. When we cast our faults with entire filial confidence into the devouring fire of love, how could these not be consumed beyond return?" (Letter of June 21, 1897. *Letters of St. Therese of Lisieux*, vol. 2, trans. J. Clarke, OCD [Washington, DC: Institute of Carmelite Studies, 1988], pp. 1133–1134).

9 2 Corinthians 12:8–10.

10 My source for the life of Edith Stein is Teresia Renata Posselt, OCD, *Edith Stein: The Life of a Philosopher and Carmelite* (Institute of Carmelite Studies: Washington, DC, 2005).

11 Romans 8:37–39.

12 See Scheffler, *Death and the Afterlife*, chapter 1.

13 I rely on Nagai's own memoir where possible: Takashi Nagai, *The Bells of Nagasaki*, trans. William Johnston (Tokyo, New York and London: Kodansha International, 1984). To fill in gaps, I rely on Glynn, *A Song for Nagasaki*.

14 Takashi Nagai, *The Bells of Nagasaki*, p. 21.

Conclusion

1 1 Corinthians 15:52.

BIBLIOGRAPHY

Aelred of Rievaulx, *De institutione inclusarum: Two English Versions*, ed. J. Ayto and A. Barratt. London and New York: Oxford University Press, 1984.

Anchoritic Spirituality: Ancrene Wisse and Associated Works, trans A. Savage and N. Watson. Mahwah, NJ: Paulist Press, 1991.

Athanasius of Alexandria, *The Life of Antony*, trans. T. Vivian and A. N. Athanassakis. Kalamazoo, MI: Cistercian Publications, 2003.

Augustine, *Confessions*, trans. F. Sheed. New York: Sheed and Ward, 1943.

Bonaventure, *The Life of Saint Francis of Assisi*, trans. B Fahey; chapters 1 and 2. In *St Francis of Assisi: Writings and Early Biographies*, ed. M. Habig. Chicago, IL: Franciscan Herald Press, 1973.

Bonniwell, Fr. William, OP, *The Life of Blessed Margaret of Castello*. Rockford, IL: TAN, 1983.

Brown, Peter, *Augustine of Hippo: A Biography*. Berkeley: University of California Press, 2013; originally published 1970.

Burrows, Ruth, *The Essence of Prayer*. Mahwah, NJ: Hidden Spring, 2006.

Cassian, John, *The Institutes*, trans. Boniface Ramsey. New York: Newman Press, 2000.

Cather, Willa, *Death Comes for the Archbishop*. New York: Knopf, 1927.

Caussade, Jean-Pierre, *Abandonment to Divine Providence*, trans. John Beevers. New York: Image, 1975.

Chesterton, G. K., *St. Francis of Assisi*. London: Hodder and Stoughton, 1924.

Ciszek, Fr. Walter, S.J., with Daniel Flaherty, SJ, *With God in Russia*. San Francisco, CA: HarperOne, 2017; originally published by America Press, 1964.

Ciszek, Fr. Walter, S.J., with Daniel Flaherty, *He Leadeth Me*. Garden City, NY: Doubleday, 1973.

Clement, Olivier, *The Song of Tears: An Essay on Repentance based on the Great Canon of St. Andrew of Crete*, trans. Michael Donley. Yonkers, NY: St. Vladimir's Press, 2021.

Dagnino, Maria Luisa, *Bakhita Tells Her Story*, 3rd ed. Rome: Casa Generalizia, Canossiane Figlie della Carità, 1993.

Dismas de Lasus, *Risques et dérives de la vie religieuse*. Paris: Editions de Cerf, 2020.

Doherty, Catherine de Hueck, *Fragments of My Life*. Notre Dame, IN: Ave Maria Press, 1979.

Doherty, Catherine de Hueck, *Poustinia: Encountering God in Silence, Solitude and Prayer*. Notre Dame, IN: Ave Maria Press, 1975.

Duquin, Lorene, *They Called Her the Baroness*. New York: Alba House, 1995.

Fanous, Daniel, *A Silent Patriarch: Kyrillos VI (1902–1971) Life and Legacy*. Yonkers, NY: St. Vladimir's Seminary Press, 2019.

Galawdewos, *The Life and Struggles of Our Mother Wallatta Petros*, trans. W. Belcher and M. Kleiner. Princeton, NJ: Princeton University Press, 2015.

Glynn, Paul, *A Song for Nagasaki*. San Francisco, CA: Ignatius Press, 1988.

Goldstein, Dawn Eden, *My Peace I Give You: Healing Sexual Wounds with the Help of the Saints*. Notre Dame, IN: Ave Maria Press, 2012.

The Grail Psalms: A New Translation. London: Collins, 1963.

Greene, Graham, *The Heart of the Matter*. New York: Penguin, 1971; originally published 1948.

Groeschel, Benedict, *The Courage to Be Chaste*. Mahwah, NJ: Paulist Press, 1985.

Guillaume de Tocco, *L'histoire de Saint Thomas d'Aquin*, trans. Claire Le Brun-Gouanvic. Paris: Éditions du Cerf, 2005.

Guinness, Alec, *Blessings in Disguise*. New York: Knopf, 1986.

Hackel, Sergei, *Pearl of Great Price: The Life of Mother Maria Skobtsova 1891–1945*. Crestwood, NY: St. Vladimir's Seminary Press, 1981.

Haflidson, Ron, *On Solitude, Conscience, Love, and Our Inner and Outer Lives*. London and New York: Bloomsbury T & T Clark, 2019.

Hart, Mother Dolores, OSB, with Richard De Neut, *The Ear of the Heart: An Actress's Journey from Hollywood to Holy Vows*. San Francisco, CA: Ignatius Press, 2013.

Hillesum, Etty, *An Interrupted Life: The Diaries 1941–1943 and Letters from Westerbork*, trans. A. J. Pomerans. New York: Henry Holt, 1996.

Hitz, Zena, *Lost in Thought: The Hidden Pleasures of an Intellectual Life*. Princeton, NJ: Princeton University Press, 2020.

Holy Women of the Syrian Orient, trans. S. Brock and S. Harvey. Berkeley and London: University of California Press, 1998.

Houselander, Caryll, *A Rocking-Horse Catholic*. New York: Sheed and Ward, 1955.

Isaac the Syrian, *The Ascetical Homilies of St. Isaac the Syrian*, revised 2nd ed. Boston: Holy Transfiguration Monastery, 2020.

Jacobus de Voraigne, *The Golden Legend: Readings on the Saints*, vols. 1 and 2, trans. William Granger Ryan. Princeton, NJ: Princeton University Press, 1993.

John of the Cross, *The Collected Works of St. John of the Cross*, trans. K. Kavanaugh and O. Rodriguez. Washington, DC:

Institute for Carmelite Studies Publications, 2017; originally published 1991.

Kenan, Randall (ed.), *James Baldwin: The Cross of Redemption: Uncollected Writings*. New York: Vintage Random House, 2010.

Kierkegaard, Søren, *Fear and Trembling*, trans. H. V. Hong and E. H. Hong. Princeton, NJ: Princeton University Press, 1983.

Kierkegaard, Søren, *Philosophical Fragments*, trans. H. V. Hong and E. H. Hong. Princeton, NJ: Princeton University Press, 1985.

Kuhse, Helga and Peter Singer (eds.), *Bioethics: An Anthology*. Oxford: Blackwell, 2006.

Lawrence, C. H., *Medieval Monasticism*, 2nd ed. London and New York: Longman, 1989.

The Life of Saint Mary of Egypt. In *The Great Canon of St Andrew of Crete and The Life of Saint Mary of Egypt*, trans. Abbes Thekla and Mother Katherine, ed. Fr Christopher Wallace. n.p.: Finnan Books, 2013, pp. 106–138.

The Lives of the Desert Fathers, trans. N. Russell. Kalamazoo, MI: Cistercian Press, 1984.

McCabe, Herbert, OP, *God Matters*. London: Chapman, 1987.

Nagel, Thomas, "The Absurd," *Journal of Philosophy* 68:20 (1971), 716–727.

Nault, Jean-Charles, OSB, *The Noonday Devil: Acedia, the Unnamed Evil of Our Times*. San Francisco, CA: Ignatius, 2013.

O'Grady, William, "The Bible and the Human Heart," *The St. John's Review* 37:1 (1986), 65–69.

Peguy, Charles, *Basic Verities*, trans. Anne and Julian Green. New York: Pantheon Books, 1943.

Posselt, Teresia Renata, OCD, *Edith Stein: The Life of a Philosopher and Carmelite*. Washington, DC: Institute of Carmelite Studies, 2005.

Raphael, Pierre, *Inside Rikers Island: A Chaplain's Search for God*. Maryknoll, NY: Orbis, 1990.

Raymond of Capua, *The Life of St. Catherine of Siena*, trans. George Lamb. Rockford, IL: Tan Books, 2003; reprint of Harvill Press and P. J. Kenedy and Sons, 1960.

Richardson, Cyril C., *Early Christian Fathers*. Philadelphia, PA: The Westminster Press, 1953.

The Rule of St. Benedict, trans. L. Dysinger. Santa Ana, CA: Source Books, 1997.

The Sayings of the Desert Fathers, trans. Benedicta Ward. Trappist, Kentucky: Cistercian Press, 1984.

Scheffler, Samuel, *Death and the Afterlife*. Oxford: Oxford University Press, 2014.

Setiya, Kieran, "The Mid-Life Crisis," *Philosopher's Imprint* 14:31 (2014), 1–18.

Setiya, Kieran, *Midlife: A Philosophical Guide*. Princeton, NJ: Princeton University Press, 2019.

Setiya, Kieran, *Life Is Hard*. New York: Penguin, 2022.

Severus, Sulpicius, *On The Life of Saint Martin*, trans. A. Roberts. In *Nicene and Post-Nicene Fathers*, Second Series, vol. 11, rev. and ed. K. Knight. www.newadvent.org/fathers/3501.htm.

Stump, Eleanore, *Wandering in Darkness*. Oxford: Oxford University Press, 2010.

Stump, Eleanore, *Atonement*. Oxford: Oxford University Press, 2018.

Takashi Nagai, *The Bells of Nagasaki*, trans. William Johnston. Tokyo, New York and London: Kodansha International, 1984; originally published, 1949.

Teresa of Avila, Foundations. In *the Complete Works of St Teresa of Jesus*, vol. 3, trans. E. Allison Peers. London and New York: Sheed and Ward, 1946, pp. 1–206.

Theodoret of Cyrrhus, *A History of the Monks of Syria*, trans. R. M. Price. Kalamazoo, MI: Cistercian Publications, 1985.

Thérèse of Lisieux, *Autobiography*, trans. Ronald Knox. New York: PJ Kenedy, 1958.

Thérèse of Lisieux, *Letters of St. Therese of Lisieux*, vol. 2, trans. J. Clarke, OCD. Washington, DC: Institute of Carmelite Studies, 1988.

Thi, Kim Phuc Phan, *Fire Road: The Napalm Girl's Journey through the Horrors of War to Faith, Forgiveness, and Peace*. n. p.: Tyndale Momentum, 2017.

Undset, Sigrid, *The Master of Hestviken*, 4 vols. trans. Arthur Chater. New York: Knopf, 1952; translation from Norwegian *Olav Audunssøn i Hestviken* (1925) and *Olav Audunssøn og hans børn* (1927).

Undset, Sigrid, *Olav Audunssøn*, vol. 1, *Vows*, and vol. 2, *Providence*, trans. Tiina Nunnally. Minneapolis, MN: University of Minnesota Press, 2020–2021; translation of *Olav Audunssøn i Hestviken* (1925).

Vodolazkin, Eugene, *Laurus*, trans. L. C. Hayden. London: Oneworld, 2015.

Ward, Benedicta, *Harlots of the Desert*. Trappist, KY: Cistercian Publications, 1987.

The Way of a Pilgrim, trans. Helen Bacovcin. New York and London: Image Doubleday, 1978.

Williams, Bernard, "The Makropoulos Case: Reflections on the Tedium of Immortality." In *Problems of the Self*. Cambridge: Cambridge University Press, 1973, 82–100.

Zanini, Roberto, *Bakhita: From Slave to Saint*. San Francisco, CA: Ignatius, 2013.

INDEX